The SECRET of NUMBERS

WHAT IS THE **HIDDEN MESSAGE** IN YOUR DATE OF BIRTH?

Monika Ben Thabetova and Andrea Tonello

Published by
Hasmark Publishing, judy@hasmarkservices.com

Disclaimer

This book is designed to provide information and motivation to our readers. It is sold with the understanding that the publisher is not engaged to render any type of psychological, legal, or any other kind of professional advice. The content of each article is the sole expression and opinion of its author, and not necessarily that of the publisher. No warranties or guarantees are expressed or implied by the publisher's choice to include any of the content in this volume. Neither the publisher nor the individual author(s) shall be liable for any physical, psychological, emotional, financial, or commercial damages, including, but not limited to, special, incidental, consequential or other damages. Our views and rights are the same: You are responsible for your own choices, actions, and results.

Permission should be addressed in writing to Monika Ben Thabetova and Andrea Tonello: Andrea Tonello, Via Chiesa n. 32 36034 MALO (VI) ITALY.

Editor
Sigrid Macdonald
sigridmacdonald@rogerscom

Cover and Book Design
Anne Karklins
annekarklins@gmail.com

Cover Photo
Fabrizio Fenucci – X Studio Milano
www.fabriziofenucci.com

First Edition, 2017

ISBN-13: 978-1-988071-44-2
ISBN-10: 1988071445

Hasmark
PUBLISHING

WHAT PEOPLE ARE SAYING
ABOUT THE SECRET OF NUMBERS

"The Secret of Numbers *is unlike any book I have ever read before... As a human being we are conditioned for greater fulfillment and fuller expression. It is your natural state to want to experience more. I truly believe this book can help you with that. I entered the secret world of numbers when I met the authors and I am so grateful that I did. I am confident you will be grateful as well.*"

  – **Peggy McColl**, *New York Times* Bestselling Author

"*I met Monika before a dramatic turning point in my life. She had already anticipated meeting me in sharp detail six months before it happened. Monika has a disconcerting ability to clarify things to those who want to trust and rely on the sensitivity of numbers... I do and I will continue to.*"

  – **Roberto Cerè**, Best Selling Author and Corporate Executive Coach

"*Monika made my numeric table and read my numbers. It was as if she was flipping through my life all the way up to the present moment... The things she said opened my heart and I felt enlightened and clear again. Since then she has become my life coach and source of support during difficult times in my life. With her help, I have achieved goals I never imagined. I won my first race in the IFBB, the prestigious Trofeo Farnese Hercules, which gave me the opportunity to represent Italy and compete in the Olympia bodybuilding competition. A dream come true!*"

  – **Manuela De Simone Esculapio**, Italian Bodybuilding Champion

"*After having read* The Secret of Numbers, *I have applied it in my life to great benefit. I've discovered strengths I had and I also learned better ways to interact with others based on their numbers. Overall, it's been very beneficial to me.*"

  – **Mick Petersen**, International Best Selling Author of
  Stella and the Timekeepers

"The Secret of Numbers *opened my eyes to a whole new world. By following the exercises in the book, I immediately learned a tremendous amount myself... and those I love. The self-clarity you can gain from this book is stunning! The Secret of Numbers is a gift. Open it, and make full use of its power.*"

  – **Casey Demchak**, Author, Award-Winning Copywriter & Consultant

Dedication

Monika –

I dedicate this book to my beloved daughters, Elisabeth and Aisha. I love you!

A special dedication goes to Jamel, a man the universe sent especially for me. He's my soul mate. The one with whom I get to grow old.

A special dedication goes to my friends Debora Bogoni, Roberto Robba, Andrea Terranova, Robin Bitto' and Alfred Dal Bianco who have supported and helped me by sharing with me their unique viewpoints on life.

Andrea –

I dedicate this book to my daughter, Arianna, the light of my life, and to Michela, one of the most important women in my life.

A sincere dedication goes out to all the people who made the decision to become proactive in their own lives. You've found the courage within yourself to change what you wanted to change and improve about yourself.

And last but not least, a final dedication goes out to all people who have a birthday!

Acknowledgements

I thank my editor.

Special thanks go to Luciano and Emma's grandparents, two special people who have welcomed me into their home with great affection. The unconditional love that they have bestowed on me has allowed me to find all the tranquility necessary to give birth to this book.

I thank my friend Manuela Pasquali, the daughter of Luciano and Emma, with whom I have always been close, even during the most difficult moments of my life. But especially during the writing of this book.

Special thanks go to Mick Petersen, for the very important support he gave us transcribing English texts. Thank you for your sensitivity, Mick!

And finally, a special thank you to two special women, Manuela and Michela, for their immense patience in reading and rereading the texts with me and Andrea, my co-author.

Table of Contents

Conclusion

The Secret Message Hidden Within the Numbers of Your Birthdate

Can knowing the numbers of your birthdate change the direction of your life? Yes, they absolutely can. Inside this book is the access code to your happiness.

After 25 years of knowing the secret contained in "your" numbers, I finally decided to share "my" message with the world. It's a heartfelt message that changed my life. And it changes the lives of those who hear, learn, and understand its significance. With this knowledge, this gift, I would like you, dear reader, to know that what is written in the following pages can have an immense impact on your life. In reality, as strange as it may sound, from the depths of my soul, I feel I was "chosen" to bring you this gift. What I'm sharing with you is actually not mine per se, but rather, I am a channel through which this message has come to be distributed to all corners of the world for the benefit of everyone. You see, every human being can benefit from THE SECRET of NUMBERS. Would you like to know what message it is that I'm talking about? The only way to interpret it is to actually read the numbers in your birthdate. The "secret" is contained within each person's date of birth.

For many years now, my heart has been yearning to help as many people as possible become aware of the significance of the energetic value of their numbers and to teach them why they are so important. As we climb up another rung on the ladder of our own personal evolutionary journey to experience a quantum leap toward our own personal "awakening," we must not only pursue happiness, peace, and harmony, but it's imperative we also seek out the power of self-control, self-reliance, and self-sufficiency. Armed with the information that follows, never again will another person have the ability to control or manipulate you. Ever. Remember – no one is easier to control than an unhappy person living in fear. And there is no one more difficult to control than a happy person living with enthusiasm, confidence, and vigor!

Foreword

When you have been around an industry for close to 40 years, as I have, you tend to see all types of materials, books, programs, offerings that are all designed to improve your life. It is extremely rare to have a book come along that, not only surprises you, but captivates you to a point of fascination. This book is precisely that book. *The Secret of Numbers* is unlike any book I have ever read before and the author is an authentic, gifted, genuine person who has a sincere desire to help you in your life. And, the gift is, the understandings in this book will help you… if you let it.

As you dive into this unique book, decide to devote uninterrupted time to really study this. You will be guided to understand what your secret numbers are and how they impact your life in every way. You will learn about a very important subject: YOU. When you truly appreciate this knowledge, your life can change in only glorious ways.

There is a lot to this. This isn't another "numerology" understanding or a version of or a type of horoscope reading that will have you giddy with excitement about meeting some strange person in an unexpected way. This is science blended with doctrine that will open your eyes to the possibilities that are awaiting your acknowledgement.

The greater you understand yourself, the greater you understand your world. There are three key ingredients that I have found to be essential for improvement. They are:

1. An open mind.
2. A willingness to improve.
3. The action required to set upon that improvement.

As a human being we are conditioned for greater fulfillment and fuller expression. It is your natural state to want to experience more. I truly believe this book can help you with that.

If you have ever watched any of my videos on YouTube or have been in one of my webinars, I often wrap up my webinar with these words: "*Have fun with it. Life is meant to be fun.*" I truly believe that. The knowledge you will gain from this book is fun. So, have fun with it and enjoy the experience of the positive life changes you are about to have.

I love this line from this book: *"If you read this book all the way through to the very end, you will enter into a world that you possibly never even imagined existed – the wonderful world of numbers. "*

I entered the secret world of numbers when I met the authors and I am so grateful that I did. I am confident you will be grateful as well.

Peggy McColl
New York Times Best Selling Author
http://PeggyMcColl.com

Introduction

This book hasn't dropped into your hands by accident. It came into your possession because you attracted it. You are somebody who has decided to challenge yourself with personal growth. I suspect you're successful, but every now and then, you have a strange and inexplicable desire to experience something bigger and better in your life. Or maybe you're facing a difficult situation, and you feel stuck. Or perhaps your life is great, but you are curious to know how and why you attract particular experiences and relationships to you. Or maybe you're one of those wonderful beings who feels a deep need to help others.

Whichever one of the above-mentioned cases applies, this book will be useful to you because:

- It will give you a new awareness.
- You'll gain knowledge that will allow you to live in a different way.
- You will learn methods that will teach you how to make the world a better place for everyone.

If you are a psychologist or psychiatrist, you have the good fortune of adding a new tool to your toolbox, enhancing those you already possess, and providing new facets to your professional practice.

If you are an employer or someone whose work puts you in contact with people every day, you will have the opportunity to acquire information that will facilitate your relationships with employees and co-workers, increasing your understanding of the strengths and weaknesses of others with whom you come in contact.

If you are a teacher or coach, the knowledge that you will acquire through this book will enable you to work with your students better, helping them to accelerate their learning in a more focused manner.

If you are a parent, you will be able to better understand your child, helping them to make better choices and find their own happiness.

If you are a numerologist, or you're interested in the world of numbers, I would ask you to try, for a moment, to suspend all previously learned knowledge about the science of numbers and numerology. Try not to compare this book to anything else you may have studied prior. Act as if this was your first exposure to this type of material. Once you've seen the way I approach numbers, feel free to integrate what you've learned here with any previous knowledge or experience at a later time, if you want. But for now, just approach the following information with an open mind. I promise it will all make sense.

And finally, if you live with someone, be it a spouse, partner, or roommate, you can finally better understand what goes through their head, allowing you to live more harmoniously together. I think this is all we really want, don't you?

Survival

Let's take a look at the world today. Every morning when you open your eyes, you get out of bed to carry on your life from where it left off the day before. But there is a bigger world out there. So what do we actually take part in?

We are, of course, part of the broader world around us. But what is it that actually surrounds us? If we are to believe the newspapers, it's war, violence, arguments, disease, sadness, confusion, suffering, and misunderstanding. Overall, there is a tremendous lack of awareness in the minds of most people.

One of the biggest problems we face as a global community today is that there are lots of people who live their lives without a true sense of what "living" really means.

Many people don't even realize they are not living or at least not in the true sense of the word. They're in survival mode. They squeak by, running like a hamster in his cage on a wheel that keeps spinning round and round. They never stop to assess their situation because if they did, they'd see that they're not going anywhere. There's rarely any questioning or self-reflection. There is no active thought as to why they're living the way they are.

If any one of us has the good fortune of realizing that there's a bigger and better way of living available, then we'd find the courage to ask bigger life questions, such as:

- "Who am I?"
- "What am I doing here?"
- "Where am I going?"
- "How do I make sense of my existence?"
- "How can I make my life a richer and more meaningful one?"
- "Am I really happy?"

These are very common questions, but... answers don't always come easily and, when they do, they're rarely clear.

Surely you agree that it would take a long time to understand the true meaning of life. It may be what unfolds moment by moment, with perseverance and patience, with love and dedication. A true understanding of the meaning of life could bring happiness where it's missing, or wealth where there's only poverty, or comfort where there's only pain.

To accomplish this, you'll need strength and energy. Don't you agree?

In order to achieve this, you must take the first step. Which step, and to what end, you ask? Achieving an awareness of always being true to yourself in any situation, as you reach for and attain a specific goal.

For Andrea and me, this is the true meaning of life.

Too many people look outside themselves for meaning in their lives. Meaning is defined by the things around them, as they race around from here to there without ever defining a precise goal. Eventually, they realize that if they continue in this manner, they will never get anywhere.

These people do not know that all the answers to their questions, all the formulas needed to be filled with life's energy, are hidden inside of them. The numbers that make up their birthdates can help them find these answers. I know it may be difficult to believe, but it's true. It's also true that you've been fed information about the significance of numbers all your life. Adults throughout our lives, both in school and at home, have understood and taught us only the functionality of the "quantum" of numbers. From an early age, the only thing you were taught was the mathematical concept of numbers, such as $1 + 1 = 2$.

Whenever you were asked, "How old are you?" you proudly held up your little fingers to show your age, and those same adults clapped enthusiastically.

In school, you learned your numbers and studied mathematics. In History class, you learned important dates. In Geography, you learned the number of inhabitants in cities and the distance between places. In Science, you were taught how to distinguish animals based on the number of legs. In Chemistry, you learned the value of formulas. In Music, you counted notes. In Physics, you measured temperatures and pressure. In fact, everything you learned about numbers revolved around their "quantum" measurement.

In your life as an adult, you have applied the same quantum knowledge that you learned as a child. You count and use numbers in your everyday reality. If you really think about it, you realize that every moment of your life is marked by numbers. Numbers account for the money in your wallet, the time on the clock, and the phone number you jot down. At a restaurant when you meet friends for dinner, numbers account for how many people are sitting at the table, how many glasses there are, and the volume of water in each. If you cook dinner at home, you must calculate how much pasta you'll need for the number of people you're having over, and on and on it goes. Just consider these simple examples from your everyday life, and reflect on the fact that behind every aspect of your life, there are numbers.

When you wake up in the morning, you open your eyes, and the first thing you look at is the clock on the bedside table that tells you the time. That number tells you it's time to get up. When you look at a thermometer it tells you the temperature outside, so you will know how to dress to be comfortable throughout the day. And so your meeting with numbers continues over the course of your day. And your day usually ends with a last peek at the clock to calculate how long you will need to sleep to get at least eight hours of sleep, which will guarantee you the proper rest.

The understanding, use, and knowledge of numbers, for most people, stops right here.

You've been taught that the only need for numbers, their only meaning, results in an amount. You have also learned to believe this to be true. The sole use you've made of numbers in your life, thus far, has been limited to this fact. Based on this, you've formed the idea that the meaning of numbers ends there as well.

Day after day, you live surrounded by these magnificent numbers without the slightest understanding of their true importance. You live without even the vaguest idea that the numbers accompanying you through life, if analyzed from a different perspective, could help you learn about yourself and others, and they can direct you to answers to questions about your existence and your purpose here on earth.

A final issue I want to mention is the lack of awareness that people have regarding who they really are. Each person has a "soul mission." The lack of contemplating this fact has progressively lead to a worldwide human identity crisis, in which we lack ideals and goals to aim for. More and more, people turn away from themselves, from their own true natures, and depend on the approval and the esteem of others without being cognizant of how unique, remarkable, and special they truly are. What people should understand is that self-esteem cannot come from someone else. The need for the approval of others is like believing that what someone else thinks of them is more important than what they think of themselves. The knowledge of one's personal identity and the recognition of the identity of others are the starting point essential to achieving what you want out of life.

The great Egyptologist Schwaller de Lubicz said: "*The evil of the West depends mostly from having accepted a mindset that is in contradiction with the thought of Nature.*" Certain materialistic sciences continue to deny the fact that, in nature, there are no experiments, only "facts." This approach denies the magical side of life, as it pertains to the invisible world in which anything is possible. A side of life where time and space do not exist, because they are constantly evolving in the here and now. That wonderful place where everything is connected to a collective and universal life force. A primordial energy. A power from which all things come. An energy that is governed exclusively by numbers.

Man is always in need of certainties, that's true. But, it's the question at the base of knowledge. Just by doubt, by questioning what until today was granted, something new can be born.

Certainty does not lead to development. The laws of nature don't allow certainty to remain in a world of knowledge, caged in by wrong patterns.

"*Freedom is not missing, free men are missing.*"

Leo Longanesi

The world is changing

Fortunately, in recent years, many "certainties" once considered true have started to crumble. People have started to understand that they can no longer cling to these crumbling certainties. This is because what was valid yesterday, today no longer is.

This type of change scares a lot of people. But looking at it from another point of view forces us to think differently than before. Nothing can be taken for granted; everything must always be challenged. And change is constant.

For 4000 years, the establishment has kept the truth about the power of numbers hidden from the masses. So in this book, we uncover what has been kept from us. Upon examination, it becomes glaringly obvious that the current theory of one of the oldest sciences in the world is incomplete. Handed down by great philosophers, scientists, and thinkers like **Pythagoras, Plato, Socrates, Leonardo da Vinci, Albert Einstein, Johannes Kepler, CG Jung, George Cantor** and many others; many of whom had concluded that numbers contained a deeper meaning with the ability to answer questions for all of humanity. We must take their forgotten theory off the shelf, dust it off, and place it back into mainstream thinking. It's time to recognize its immense importance and accuracy by shedding light on it once again.

Why is this so important to you as an individual? Because it can help you improve yourself and your life by awakening your soul. The process is a valuable tool with an accuracy rate above 99% when applied to any individual.

The positive aspect of doing this will bring to life new ideas, new thinking, new concepts, and new theories with a crystal clear focus.

Included as part of the information Monika discovered is an ancient table that was lost for many generations but has existed for thousands of years. Her interpretation of this table, which is filled in by using a special process calculated with the numbers from a person's date of birth, is a powerful tool from which comes a powerful new self-awareness and a deeper understanding of the people in our lives. It is a simple, fast, and totally understandable process we call THE SECRET of NUMBERS.

Every one of us experiences beautiful, happy times in our own lives. In living these moments, we feel strong, energetic, beautiful, safe, and above all, we think that nothing could possibly change the situation. Then something happens suddenly, unexpectedly, and we find ourselves in the middle of a difficult situation where we feel weak, insecure, misunderstood, or alone. When we feel like this, we close ourselves off to the outside world without asking for help. THE SECRET of NUMBERS table has the ability to give you the necessary help you'll need for tackling these dark moments in your life in a different way.

I cannot say that my life is all rainbows and unicorns now. However, I am much more confident than ever before, because I use THE SECRET of NUMBERS table. I now look at life through a different lens. Let's face it; much of our pain, very often, is linked to other people. But with the help of the table, we'll be able to look at any situation, at any person, and even at ourselves differently. It leads us to have greater inner clarity, reach better decisions, or take more positive actions. Because of this new approach to life, each of us can regain the feeling of having true freedom and happiness.

One of the other benefits to using the table is the ability to understand difficulties that arise in our lives and to actually recognize them as opportunities from which a path of growth and spiritual evolution emerges. Instead of complaining about them, we will begin to bless and thank these challenges that life presents to us every day.

At times we, unfortunately, let our emotions manipulate us, control us, making us feel trapped or chained to the feeling of being stuck. Have you ever noticed that the most significant changes in your life, those which lead you to a higher level of consciousness, are born from an awareness of overcoming great pain or deep sorrow? In the end, your new, higher consciousness frees you from the chains, and then, once again, you have the ability to open your wings and fly. It feels like your freedom has been restored.

"Change does not mean that we lose our way;
rather it means that we take a new path.
We make the commitment to live a life inspired by purpose,
instead of endless claims and false promises
which are a sign of the ego badge."
Wayne W. Dyer

What you REALLY need

Yes, at last, one of the oldest methods that has helped people for thousands of years to experience a more serene and peaceful life is coming back among us once again! Isn't that wonderful news?

With help from the table of THE SECRET of NUMBERS, you can figure out what you REALLY need to find the right balance that allows you the ability to reflect on your inner potential and use it in a constructive way to feel at ease with yourself and with others.

Never again will you be manipulated by the false beliefs and poor conditioning in your mind and from your emotions. You will finally be able to return to your true essence and be your true self.

This is because this wonderful table provides the key for accessing specific information about the unique and unrepeatable individual "mechanics" of every single person, including psychology, health, talent, strengths, weaknesses as well as special gifts.

I hope you can understand the power of dialing in directly, so that you find your own specific purpose along with a "roadmap" for your life.

The meeting of two minds

Our bodies, our thoughts, our emotions, and everything around us is energy. Everything, every person, every situation that we have manifested in our lives, we attracted, because we were both vibrating on the same frequency. For this reason, I am convinced that there is no case where someone shows up in our lives who we don't require as a guide. The universe sent them to teach us something, because we needed the lesson.

The case is the same in regards to the relationship between Andrea and me. I won't divulge all the details at this point since it's written in Andrea's story later in the book. Instead, I want to tell you about two people who were born in different countries, with different skin tones, and from different cultures. We could never have planned our meeting on our own. We met because of divine intervention.

Andrea Tonello was born in 1975 in a town called Malo in the province of Vicenza, Italy. For as long back as anyone could remember, everyone in his family made a living as a barber or a hairdresser. But thanks to his incredible strength of will and determination, Andrea broke the family pattern despite the strong opposition and lack of support from his father. Instead, he became a lawyer, eventually opening up his own law practice, which thrived from day one. Being financially successful gave him everything he thought he ever wanted. However, years later, Andrea experienced an "awakening" that lead him to realize that in spite of having "everything," he felt like he actually had nothing.

Monika Ben Thabetova was born in 1976 in the second largest city of the Czech Republic named Brno. Her family was of a multi-ethnic origin. After stints of living in Africa and the Czech Republic, she settled in Italy. At the age of 15, her mother introduced her to the table of THE SECRET of NUMBERS. After a short amount of time, it became apparent that she had an uncanny ability to uniquely interpret the ancient instrument. And so began her daily use of it to help the people around her.

Two unique stories that differ completely, but, thanks to the universal law of attraction, our meeting was inevitable.

At the beginning of our friendship, we confessed to one another that, in fact, as kids, we had always felt different from everyone else in some indefinable way. We struggled to adapt to everyday life. Children, as well as adults, bullied us, because we didn't accept the futures that our parents and society had proposed for us. Instead, we blazed our own trails forward despite all the opposition against us.

Both of us had contentious pasts which, thanks to our inner strength, we overcame.

As we told each other our life stories, we realized that each of us had experienced very similar childhoods. Years of listening to an internal voice from dawn to dusk that encouraged us to hold on. We determined that what we had gone through was just a test of endurance. That voice also shared with us that the life we knew was more than it appeared to be. We held fast to the belief that there was more to it. We both felt we were born into this world to accomplish a great mission, not just eat, sleep and "get by." We were convinced that we had both come into this life for something more important than the life that was laid out for us. Neither of us knew what that mission was, but we kept our feelings secret. Time passed. And our lives moved along uneventfully until our fateful meeting in 2014.

One day, while hiking through a beautiful forest surrounded by nature, Andrea said, "I have decided I want to help you spread your message, the unique way in which you interpret numbers, all over the world. I'm convinced that it is my mission to help you with yours."

That day, he also expressed how my interpretation of his birthdate using the table from THE SECRET of NUMBERS had changed his life. For this reason, he felt compelled to help me bring "enlightenment" for the benefit of as many people as possible. It is here that our true "soul mission" began.

First as individuals, then as a team, we decided that the time had come to share our message with the world. Using our knowledge and experience, our mission became clear: to awaken and elevate people's consciousness. We wanted to bring people to self-awareness, to help change the pain, loneliness, and unconsciousness of the people of the Earth.

Actually, dear reader, it is thanks to Andrea that you are now reading these lines. Because without his help, it would have been next to impossible for me to make this happen alone.

Do you know that you can?

No one's life was ever "easy." Every one of us has had to overcome great difficulties. But going forward, our task becomes easier with the assistance of THE SECRET of NUMBERS table. Equipped with this table, the knowledge we gain about ourselves is incredible.

Andrea and I are confident that through the information you will get out of this book, you will achieve a new awareness of yourself and an understanding of who you really are; from there, you'll be able to begin your new life path. Change will frighten you no longer, and you will be able to face setbacks and challenges with peace in your heart and with the elegance of a confident adult, not with sadness and the despair of a frightened child. You will find within yourself the strength to start that new project or that new job, to write down new goals, to realize a lifelong dream, or to continue doing what you were already doing but with a bigger smile on your face. And the best part is that people around you will perceive this change in you too. You may even influence them positively, becoming a good example for them to make some personal changes too.

The single best thing any of us can do is contribute our knowledge and experience to improve the lives of other people, allowing us to somehow leave a beautiful impression on them. Remember that even stars can shine without darkness.

The wonderful world of numbers

If you read this book all the way through to the very end, you will enter into a world that you possibly never even imagined existed – the wonderful world of numbers.

You will discover that many of your doubts will disappear as the answers to your deepest questions rise to the surface. It is possible that you will begin living with a renewed sense of vitality as if you were beginning a chapter in your life and the lives of those around you. It's a bit like changing the lens on a camera: everyone around you begins to look different – better, sharper, and more in focus. It will be like you removed their masks, and their true essence came through for the first time. Any artifice of appearance, superficiality, or façade will vanish into thin air.

Because when we live in a reality of superficiality without following a true flow of self, inauthentic situations arise in our lives. A feeling of heaviness, a kind of power failure shows up to make our lives a constant struggle. It would feel like we are forever swimming upstream against the current. Have you ever tried standing still in a river as the water flows forcefully past your legs? It's a task of near impossibility that takes remarkable effort on your part just to maintain your balance. In the end, unfortunately, your efforts are wasted since you wouldn't withstand the rushing current. You would eventually topple over and be whisked off down the river. From a defeat of this nature, people may tend to get angry with themselves, and this anger manifests itself as negative emotions that don't take into account any of the underlying reasons that created the situation in the first place. When we don't go with the "flow," it is generally because we're afraid of what we might encounter. Perhaps memories from our past that caused us to experience great pain play a part. We are constantly influenced by an expectation of what our futures might hold, and our previous pain weighs in on that expectation. Our heads go to that place without us even realizing it. It always seems to go in two directions, into two worlds. The truth is that neither our expectations of the future nor our pain from the past exists in reality – they're only in our minds. When we live in this type of mental chaos, even our bodies are affected, becoming weaker and sick.

This status always takes us farther away from our spiritual source. We must instead learn to be transported by life's flow, to adhere to the life force, and to follow our own inner guidance system.

The healthier and more vital our bodies, the more relaxed and clear our minds will become. And the more complete we will feel, both spiritually and emotionally.

Where do we travel?

In the first chapter, I will address the problems of today's society and especially speak of my personal development experience. You read my brief personal story and Monika's as well.

In the second chapter, we will reveal the extraordinary numbers reading system and show you how to interpret the ancient table of THE SECRET of NUMBERS. We will also share with you the stories of some of the people who've experienced and benefitted from interpreting their numbers on the table.

In the third chapter, we will tie up all the loose ends. We will give you our website and ways to get in touch with us for deepening your understanding of numbers. But only if you want it! There will be many other opportunities for us to meet again. I will give a more comprehensive explanation at the end of the book.

Although I've already written this, I would like to emphasize again what you'll learn:

- You will learn to react differently to situations that life inevitably hands you, because you will be able to use the powerful tool that allows you to read people on a deeper level, beyond what you see in their appearance.

- You will learn to better understand your partner, your children, your colleagues at work, your boss, your customers and, in general, everybody with whom you come into in contact on your journey.

- You will finally gain the necessary tools to figure out whether a person is fit to be your partner, your spouse, your employer, your employee or client, an acquaintance or a good friend.

By the end of the book, we hope you will have learned the basic interpretation of the table of THE SECRET of NUMBERS. If you do, it will allow you to gain a new awareness of yourself and of those around you and to interact with them in new and different ways.

Each goodbye, every change, every hardship, every moment of happiness, each course attended, and every book read will teach you new things that will only get better with your true essence and will help you understand more about own UNIQUENESS.

What is Oneness?

I want to focus on this word – Oneness. No one really understands or comprehends who he is or why he must discover his individual uniqueness.

But first, let's ask another question – how can you discover your own uniqueness if you don't know who you really are at your core? Everybody says, "*I am so and so.*" Or "*I am this way or that.*" Or "I *have done such and such*"... but what does that mean? We must first know who we are to become so and so, or this and that, or such and such. It's imperative to first know what we want, but most people go through life without having a clue. It seems everyone knows what he doesn't want, which leads to what he does not want to happen. So we must first figure out what we want. Then we can know who we are. But you ask, "how do I find out who I really am?" It's a tough thing to figure out. The first thing you must do is ask yourself the right questions, powerful questions, in order to get any answers at all. With patience, persistence and time, the answers will come. But if you answer impulsively, it may be your paradigms (habits that are formed based on causes and conditions of your upbringing) answering. We are what we are, and what we are at any given moment is the result of what we have been in the past. So if we say "... *I did this* ...", we're just repeating the conditioning from our past. In truth, we aren't made in any particular way; we are actually of our own making. If we understood that we get to choose exactly how we wish to be, and we knew about our uniqueness, it would eliminate our limitations and free us of all limiting constraints. Understanding our uniqueness means realizing that we all have a unique, indispensable, and important place in the universe. Without us, nothing could exist. We are the source, and we are one with the universe.

Reality itself is a product of our thoughts. Each of us, by virtue of our thinking, helps to create the world around us. A key way to understanding our uniqueness is to figure out who we are and what we want. The moment we decipher this, a new life forms, a new existence unfolds, and a new world is born. And this is the world that lies ahead of us. It's a life that could be really wonderful.

Every person, every situation, and every thing you meet in your life is good for something.

Chapter One

Today's world

Ancient secrets have been kept hidden from most of humanity. Other secrets have been revealed only to a select few who had to first be initiated by means of participating in an occult ritual. Still others were unveiled and used to help change the lives of millions of people.

What Monika reveals in this book is just her interpretation of one of mankind's oldest secrets. This knowledge was passed down to her by her mother. For years, she practiced and perfected it. Over the course of many years, her vast life experiences have shaped and molded "her" system.

Many times, in fact, Monika has had to face enormous difficulties, both physically and psychologically, in her life. However, the table of THE SECRET of NUMBERS helped her overcome these personal challenges such that, if she had not had this kind of support, she most likely would not have even been able to get where she is today.

Equipped with her understanding of numbers, Monika is now in a position to better understand herself and the people in her life. Over time, she has learned to manage change, even when it's of the most radical nature.

Having a different awareness has enabled her to stay in a positive mental state of mind and have an inner harmony, even when it appears a storm has been unleashed.

Every day, life presents each of us with new challenges, difficulties, problems, and obstacles. Sometimes they appear at the point when we're only one foot from our goal, moments away from its arrival. It almost seems like life is making fun of us.

The normal way the majority of people react to these types of events is negatively.

Some of us get angry, others give up, while others fall into a deep depression.

Some, however, who are equipped with a greater awareness and who are just a few steps ahead of us on the evolutionary path, understand that in any challenge or with any difficulty, there lies a hidden secret passage that allows them to rise even higher, to an even higher level of awareness.

Each of us is, at this very moment, at a certain point in our evolutionary journey.

The great psychologist Wayne Dyer said: *"You're not a human being who is going through a spiritual experience. You are a spiritual being who is living a human experience."*

We are not our bodies. We aren't even our minds. We are eternal spiritual beings. Our body is lent to our spirit, allowing us to have an earthly experience from which to grow spiritually. It may seem strange, almost paradoxical, but, believe me, it is not. For we should understand that the purpose of our existence is to experience the experiences that cause us to move forward in terms of our spiritual and evolutionary growth.

Sometimes the living of many lives is required for us to evolve to the next, higher level. What do I mean by "higher level?" The universal matrix, God, the universe, call it as you see fit, always meaning the Original Source of All.

If we don't evolve, the universe forces us to repeatedly experience the same subtle challenges, the same sort of difficulties, with the objective of elevating us to the next spiritual plane as we continue on our evolutionary path.

And occasionally, it happens that the universe decides to send us a little gift to help us find our way.

This help is of utmost importance. It's not only useful for any of us who missed a fork in the road of life, but it's vitally significant for those of us who walk the "straight and narrow." Because this help can give us insight, allowing us to see a new direction, a new path, a better solution than anything we may have known previously.

This "self-analysis tool" method, which Monika is going to teach you, as long as you have the tenacity to get to the end, will open up a new dimension for you. It will provide access to a new awareness of the most intimate and deepest part of your soul. Yes, that's right! Unlike your body and mind, which are intended to be born and die after life, your spiritual being is infinite and immortal with unlimited potential.

You must understand that before your birth, you decided on your birthday; you chose with a clear intention. Although perhaps you were not aware of this. Know that when you decided to be reincarnated in your present body, your soul decided that it would live this life with a specific mission. The problem is that many people spend their whole lives unconscious to this fact. They never bothered to look for their soul's purpose, thus remaining at the same level as if they were in a video game unable to move up to the next level. Nothing in life happens by chance, not even the numbers that make up your birthdate.

I know it may seem strange, but, as mentioned in the preceding pages, up until now, families, schools, and society have taught us to look only at the quantity of numbers, not at their invisible side, their quality side, their esoteric side, their occult side.

I would like to dwell for a second on what the esoteric and the occult are.

Esotericism – *derived from the Greek esoterikos (inside, inside) is a general term for the secrecy doctrines whose teachings are meant to be "initiated" to those who are entrusted with the possibility of the revelation of the hidden truth.*

Occult – *that which is hidden, hidden, not visible.*

Initiation – *an individual must symbolically die to be reborn as a superior being. Then he's thought to be something that he really is not, and we must face a process of disidentification. What is ceases; therefore, what exists dies and so, in fact, makes space for what he really is. The person is born again.*

In the following pages, there's a detailed explanation of what Monika intends to explain about numbers – the quantitative and the qualitative sides. Her explanation will help you understand that the world of numbers is an immense one, and the world of numbers in which you have lived until now is nowhere close to what actually exists.

How things have changed

Fortunately, things have changed, because we have the ability to access knowledge that had previously been hidden from us for centuries. Can you imagine why it was hidden, protected, and almost forbidden?

Because it was considered dangerous! Yes, dangerous, but for whom?

Not for the people. If everyone suddenly became aware of who they really were, knowing that we're all unique beings with infinite potential and with specific missions to accomplish, each of us would be able to progress on our evolutionary path without being manipulated by society's system.

What counts for the system, of course, is maintaining the *status quo*, to ensure that people obey without creating problems and that they do everything they are told to do.

If someone opposes or refuses to carry out the system's program, it creates a problem that must somehow be resolved.

This is the real reason why the powers that be have always been opposed to the fact that certain knowledge should be disclosed to humanity. In this way, once the level of general awareness is raised considerably, people, knowing who they really are deep down, would feel free to rebel.

Unfortunately, there are, and there always will be, people "at the top" who don't want the "truth" disclosed. This is despite the fact that for thousands of years, this knowledge was available, was reliable, and helped people. If we think of the past history, Galileo Galilei had to remain in the shadows, and it was not possible to publish his findings, because it would go against the beliefs of the Church; Copernicus was forced to be closed, hidden in a tower when he was studying his "heliocentric theory," as his "everything revolves around the sun" contradicted the "everything revolves around the Earth" theory of the time.

Today, you too will have the chance to gain a new awareness of who you really are and thus become free; free to live and follow your soul's true mission without anyone else telling you what to do or not to do, what to think or what not think.

Now you can finally be free, free from all those invisible chains that have tied you down without even realizing it. Free from a belief system perpetuated by your family, school, or religion.

Today you can see that you're confined by a self-imposed, invisible prison, and you get to decide whether to leave it or not.

This involves a considerable effort on your part, because the most difficult chains to break are those you cannot see.

• • •

The world of numbers today

The great minds of the past realized the importance of this valuable tool, and they realized that numbers are the source of answers for all humanity.

The deeper meaning that lies behind every number has never been taught in schools, except in the Pythagorean. Although few are aware, in 532 BC, the great Pythagoras had in his school in Crotone, Italy, two classes of students. In one, he taught classical mathematics, the arithmetic we all know, and in another class, he taught only to a few chosen ones. In that one, he taught the other side of the numbers: their invisible part, the one that carries the most significance, as we have said, esoteric but at the same time more important: the qualitative meaning of each number.

Now you will discover how numbers should look, live, and feel in order for you to interpret and understand the important messages they want to convey to us. First, you have to understand the difference in perception between the quantity and the quality of a number.

Quantity of numbers

- It is the numerical value of the quantity $1 + 1 = 2$.

- The numbers you count and calculate.

- You approach with logical thinking related to the brain, and the brain leads to doubt.

- It corresponds to **linear thinking** – thinking, that is, that focuses only on one thing, something that absorbs all its attention (if we move into prehistory, man went hunting focusing on a single goal: feeding his family).

- It corresponds to **Western thought**. The capacity of introspection involves an inner journey, and because of that, you learn to look inside. You perform the evaluations, you examine the reality, and the universe gives an opinion.

- **KRONOS** – indicating time in its dimensions of past, present, and future, or the passing of the hours, minutes, and seconds.

- **TIME** refers to the sequential, logical, and quantitative (the ancient Greeks had at least three ways to indicate time).

- We approach with the Left hemisphere – where we think in words; where the conscious mind dwells; where we think using the head.

Quality number

- Digital content, character, idea.

- Numbers tell stories about life.

- We approach with intuitive understanding and with feeling.

- It corresponds to **circular reflection** – the mind is able to perform more tasks and diversify them with each other. (Think back to prehistoric humans; while men hunted, women remained in the cave, focusing on several things at once: looking after children, cooking, cleaning.)

- It corresponds to the **Eastern thought, which is** connected to the ability to see beyond the observation. It trains us to look out, not to give an assessment, and not to judge. We welcome the message, the attitude to be able to see things from different perspectives and viewpoints.

- **KAIROS** – indicating the opportune time, a good opportunity, the right moment. The ancient Greeks called it "God's time." It means "time in half." The time in which something of quality or something special happens. Growth and maturation of a fruit, the gestation of a living being. Unfortunately, Kairos always lost to Kronos, because man always preferred to follow the mind over the heart.

• We approach with the right hemisphere – where we think in pictures; where the subconscious mind dwells; where we think with our heart.

Just by reading the first few pages of this book, you have already learned one of the most important pieces of information that has been hidden from mankind for centuries. The fact that each number has not only a quantitative meaning (1 + 1 = 2) but that every single number has a specific qualitative meaning, which goes far beyond the mere mathematical aspect. Monika's first book, *1, 2, 3 Let's Talk about You!*, is centered around this subject. In it, she explains in detail the meaning behind each number. In the following pages of this book, we will go even more in depth regarding other essential components about the meaning of each number. We will give you an overview of the information contained in the first book. If, however, you read the first book (currently only available in Italian), regard the following information simply as a recap. As is said in Latin: "*repetita iuvant*," which means repeating does good.

Here are some excerpts from Monika's first book

First, I'll teach you how to add the first little sum of your date of birth.

Tools you'll need:

• a pen

• a piece of paper

• a birthdate

Let's call this first calculation your "Personal Number." I'll use a random date as the first example, so you can get a feel for how it's done. Once you understand the mechanism of how it's done, you'll be able to perform calculations on your own birthdate as well as that of anyone else about which you are interested to know more.

To find out your "Personal Number," you add the day, month, and year together. After calculating the sum, if the number is greater than 9, you'll add those digits together until the resulting number is a single digit between 1 and 9. That single number is the number of your life.

Let's see an example:

A person was born May 30, 1976.

Here's how you do it.

Add up the numbers that pertain to the day, month and year: $3 + 0 + 0 + 5 + 1 + 9 + 7 + 6 = 31$.

Now add $3 + 1 = 4$

The personal number of life in this case is the number 4.

In this "branch" of numerology, the figure must be reduced to a single digit.

Here's another example:

January 26, 2016

$0 + 1 + 2 + 6 + 2 + 0 + 1 + 6 = 18$

Now add $1 + 8 = 9$

The personal number of life in this case is the number 9.

Now you try it yourself, using your own date of birth.

IMPORTANT NOTE: There are a few exceptions to the "single digit rule." If the resulting calculation is represented by the numbers 11, 22, 33, 44, $(1 + 1 = 2)$, $(2 + 2 = 4)$, $(3 + 3 = 6)$, $(4 + 4 = 8)$, these are called "Master Numbers." Their energy is very strong, double that of the other numbers. In this book, however, you should add them up to obtain a single number between 1 and 9, as outlined earlier. As a final issue, I will give meaning to "Master Numbers." If you want to better understand those individuals who have a master number as their personal number of life, it is necessary for you to also read the meaning of the previous two single digits. For example, if your personal number is 11, after adding them together, you get a 2. In the section about the meaning of each individual number, you must read both 1 and 2.

Every number that makes up a birthdate can be read both individually and in relation to other numbers. Additional counts allow you to enter into an even deeper understanding of each individual. This is done by entering the date numbers, and those resulting from the calculations, into the 16 boxes of the table of "THE SECRET of NUMBERS." This will be explained in Chapter Two.

Here are excerpts of the basic meanings of personal numbers from 1-9

The qualitative meaning of Number 1

(Male, the head number, thinker)

Creative
Self-confident in your own value

Your creative energy has great strength and flows continuously.

With each breath, your strength is sensed by others.

This energy has the power to create good but also to destroy.

Do you use your powerful energy to direct your life?

Is there something blocking your creativity, or does it flow freely?

How does it manifest itself in a positive way?

How does it manifest itself in a negative way?

What kind of life would you have if your creativity was allowed to flow freely?

Meaning of life

People who live with the vibration of the number 1 have the mission of bringing their creative energy to the lives of others. They must, however, overcome the tendency to be overly self-critical and abandon the uncertainty about their own abilities. If self-doubt is allowed to creep in, they risk blocking this energy or using it in a negative way. Number 1's should understand that it's okay to integrate, but they must keep in mind their uniqueness, stay true to their ideas, and follow their hearts.

Strengths: creative power, charisma, authority, independence, economic success, desire, resolution, innovation, passion, study skills and assimilation of concepts, a sense of responsibility, spirit of innovation, trendsetting.

Points to ponder: loneliness, dependence, fear of failure, prejudices, hyperactivity, arrogance, self-pity, persistence, sense of inferiority, lack of confidence.

Talents: Number 1 people absolutely need to work where they can use their creativity and where they can express themselves freely.

Dancing, writing, drawing, singing, art, sports wherein they can express their creativity, consulting, designing, teaching, healing.

The qualitative meaning of Number 2

(Female, a head number, thinker)

Collaboration and balance

Did you know that before you can have the ability to become someone else's friend that you must first become friends with yourself?

Look in the mirror: you have two hands, two legs, two eyes. Why do you think there are two of each?

Because you have to work with both sides of the body, not just one.

With your two hands, one is open, and the other closed.

Which of your two hands metaphorically "offers" more?

With which do you most often say, "YES" or "NO"?

Are you more comfortable with giving or receiving?

Do you often give too much and feel empty afterward?

Have you found your "true center" in life?

Are you aware that where your responsibility ends, your "true center" begins?

Meaning of life

People who live with the vibration of the number 2 have the mission of learning to cooperate with others, but, more importantly, with themselves. They should find the limit of their responsibility toward others. They should learn how to find an inner balance of using the head and the heart. Then, once that balance has been achieved, use it to collaborate with others. Learn how to use two halves of a whole. When two opposites find one another, then it's easy to find the center.

Strengths: idealism, intuition, creativity (plenty of ideas...), sense of purpose, empathy, mediation skills, coordination skills, collaboration, negotiation skills, ability to integrate, ability to distinguish.

Points to ponder: ambiguity, fear of conflict, intolerance, liabilities, misunderstanding, mental block, mental instability, indecisive, excesses, hopelessness, insecurity, dependence.

Talents: Their largest predisposition is in their ability to collaborate. They are very effective in helping and assisting others. Great ambition often places them in leadership roles.

Teaching, coaching, functioning in important international trade positions, leading, collaborating, and volunteering.

The qualitative meaning of Number 3

(Male, heart number, communicator)

Expression and sensitivity

Imagine being a beautiful and fragrant red rosebud. Feel that inside. You are full of emotions and beautiful feelings that you would like to share with the entire world.

You want to expend your beautiful fragrance, show off your bright colors, and display your open petals. But if your petals are closed to the sun, the world will never see you. You doubt that your scent or your color would ever find favor in someone else's eyes. How important are the doubts you have about yourself?

Do you express your feelings openly, or do you tend to hide inside the bud?

Meaning of life

The way of people born with life number 3 is to positively exploit their deep emotional feelings and learn to express them with complete sincerity, first with themselves, then with others. Only by doing this can they heal their extreme sensitivity and tendency to doubt themselves.

Strengths: originality, communication through the heart, flexibility, predictability, connection with thought, ability to work in teams, spontaneity, charm, sense of humor, generosity, compassion, sense of reality.

Points to ponder: prideful, a tendency to manipulate, critical attitude, laziness, closed-mindedness, impulsivity, speculation, perfectionism, excessive self-criticism, arrogance, defensive attitude, destructive thoughts.

Talents: The creativity of number 3 people can be expressed with song, in drawing, by acting, or through the written or spoken word. They can be very good journalists, writers, teachers, and counselors. Usually, their expression starts in front of one other person but can quickly grow into groups, large or small. But when they acquire greater mastery in the art and their self-confidence blooms, they absolutely need an audience to stay healthy.

Singing, drawing, painting, acting, writing, teaching, counseling.

The qualitative meaning of the Number 4

(Female, belly number, emotional)

Stability and procedure

Imagine a big, beautiful house. How do you build a house? First, the idea is formed. Then plans are laid, and a design is sketched. It is brought into the material world once the blueprints are drawn up. Physically, the building starts at the bottom (the foundation), and then, it rises up all the way to the roof. A tried and true process must be followed.

The construction of this house resembles how your life must be built.

Isn't it a good idea to first think the whole thing through from start to finish?

Isn't it also a good idea to begin by building a strong, stable foundation, with everything?

Doesn't it always make sense to progress one step at a time to get where you want to go?

Meaning of life

The way of life for Number 4 people is to understand that they will find stability only when they follow the right procedure to attain their goal.

They should learn that the best way to succeed is to follow a step by step method. It is also important to dig a deep and sturdy foundation for them to feel confident in the finished product. Much like a tree that may have branches reaching skyward, only if its roots are strong and deep. In order for number 4's to have the best in life, they need to learn to balance body, mind, and emotion.

Strengths: logical thinking, originality, self-discipline, honesty, awareness of their purpose, working efficiency, confidence, sense of order, reliability, awareness of the abundance that exists around them, creativity, willpower, common sense, communication skills, sense of humor.

Points to ponder: uncertainty, closing, perfectionism, desire for wealth, laziness, materialism, fear of loss, intolerance, hardship, dissatisfaction, emotional instability.

Talents: People who live with the vibration of the number 4 can take advantage of their excellent communication skills in the business world. Their natural abilities make them very adept at creating organizations, such as corporations, businesses, or companies. They are also great organizers. Ideally, they're placed in job positions where they have direct access to a leader. Their great practical sense, analytical capacity, order, and reliability mark them as great motivators. It is easy for them to encourage and empower others to give their best. They also find it natural to help others overcome obstacles and setbacks.

Real estate agents, salespeople, coaches, motivational speakers, organizers, secretaries, lawyers, business people, managers, analysts.

The qualitative meaning of Number 5

(Male, the number of feet, vital)

Freedom and discipline

Imagine you're a butterfly, flying from flower to flower and living in complete freedom.

In your opinion, what do you think would test this butterfly's sense of freedom?

The only obligation a butterfly has that inhibits its freedom is when it must choose a plant to lay its eggs.

With this type of discipline, the butterfly comes in contact with another kind of freedom: to know there are priorities in life that supersede its freedom.

How do you feel emotionally when you're free?

And what kind of freedom do you feel?

And how are your emotions when you feel locked up?

Meaning of life

The way of life of number 5 people is to understand that the only way they can find freedom is through self-discipline, concentration, and by the depths of their experiences. External interferences have no influence on them and won't affect their lives. However, they must discover their own true freedom by searching within.

Strengths: enthusiasm, love, dynamism, sense of justice, communication, optimism, organizational skills, adaptability, curiosity, sense of freedom, spontaneity, adventurous spirit, open-mindedness, awareness of the value of life.

Points to ponder: rivalry, superficiality, injustice, inactivity, pride, destructiveness, boredom, addiction, victimization, stiffness, fear of conflict, separation, forgetting about themselves, a tendency of being regressive, desire to play: positive if conscious, less positive if they live without awareness.

Talents: Numbers 5's learn and understand quickly. They have a good visual imagination with a great capacity toward clairvoyance, which they must learn to use, harness correctly, and trust in their "sixth sense." When they learn to use it effectively, they will excel in professions where they're in service to others, such as doctors, lawyers, instructors, and teachers. They're capable of great imagination, and oftentimes, they see things from unusual perspectives, which are owed to their deep life experience. They are suitable for work involving movement.

Doctor, lawyer, instructors, and teachers.

The qualitative meaning of the Number 6

(Women, the number of feet, vital)

Acceptance and idealism

Your idealism directs your life or the rules?

Do you accept yourself and others around you as they are, or do you judge them according to your own self-imposed idealistic parameters?

Can you see the immense beauty of imperfection? Of perfection?

What is your vision? Can you put it into practice?

Can you see life's beauty, or do you get lost in the thought of how it would be if it were different?

Do you know how to enjoy the present moment?

Meaning of life

What is essential for people with the life number 6 is to harmonize their noble ideals with the practical reality of the everyday. Thanks to their extensive idea of natural perfection in the world, they will have to learn to accept themselves and the world around them in order to be able to connect and experience the present moment.

Strengths: idealism, loyalty, love, personal commitment, friendliness, willingness to take risks, sexual energy, spontaneity, sense of enterprise, breadth of outlook, sense of abundance, a sense of responsibility, self-reliance, motivation, sense of family.

Points to ponder: excessive control, intolerance, fear of failure, impatience, laziness, restlessness, rushed, aggression, inability to make decisions, apathy, isolation, overload, waste management, loss of guidance.

Talents: Number 6's need a job in which they can exploit their talent of always making the best of each situation, even when they're thrown into completely different and new environments. In reality, they do not perceive their job as a job but rather as a real mission. They possess the ability to transform people and ideas which, because of their high standards, can bring about excellent results.

Coaching, writing, consulting, teaching, and organizing.

The qualitative meaning of the Number 7

(Male, the number of feet, vital)

Trust and openness

Close your eyes and imagine your grandmother's jewelry box with a beautiful shiny diamond ring.

With this diamond comes a brilliant light of wisdom.

But the diamond is hidden inside the jewel box, because on its own, it doesn't perceive its own magnificent beauty or how this beauty could be shared with others. In many ways, it is afraid of being seen because it is fearful of being destroyed!

Do you sympathize with this beautiful diamond?

Meaning of life

Number 7 people must start by trusting the light of their own spirits and in the process of life's continuous development. They should begin to trust so much that they're able to finally feel safe. With this safety, they'll be able to open up to others and share their glorious inner light. The most important thing is to learn how to become more confident and open toward themselves and others.

Strengths: sensitivity, economic capacity, discipline, willingness to help, optimism, goal achievement, personality, teaching skills, hope, generosity, patience, diligence, joy of life, independence, focus on their health.

Points to ponder: impulsiveness, greed, materialism, reticence, challenging behavior, meanness, fear of defeat, emotional isolation, insecurity, jealousy, callousness, naïveté, pessimism, willingness to fight.

Talent: Number 7's have remarkable intelligence. They have an uncanny ability to grasp concepts immediately. They could read a book and very quickly comprehend it fully, even subtle "between the lines" nuances. With their special flair, they have a knack for writing and an overall good artistic predisposition. It's always their preference to work alone. In reality, with the solid reputation they have accumulated over the years, number 7's can easily function in roles at the highest level. The most important thing to remember about number 7's is that they cannot be left with free time for themselves.

Philosopher, scientist, thinker, dancer, singer, musician.

The qualitative significance of the Number 8

(Female, belly number, emotional)

Abundance and power

Imagine a glittering treasure chest full of pearls, gold, silver, and diamonds.

From this chest, you can take anything you want, and you can share the booty with anybody in your life.

How would you feel the first moment you saw this treasure chest and its glittering treasure?

What feeling would you have in knowing that you could take as much of the jewels as you wanted?

How would you feel if you discovered that this treasure already existed within you?

Meaning of life

People with life number 8 must understand that it's imperative to learn to share with others the abundance bestowed upon them by the universe. It's the only way they'll be able to earn power and recognition from others. Characterized by this strength, they can then bring well-being to themselves and to those around them. Words of importance to number 8's are money, power, authority, recognition, and control.

Strengths: managerial talent, sense of responsibility, love for people, spirituality, authority, autonomy, charm, sensuality, self-esteem, creativity, leadership, ability to unite different cultures, ability to negotiate, robustness.

Points to ponder: pricing, emotional blocks, pride, frustration, repetition, self-centeredness, fear of failure, impulsivity, pessimism, fussiness, frivolity, isolation, hunger for power, inability to gain respect, materialism.

Talents: They are led to become great financial experts, traders, large entrepreneurs, managers, team leaders. Because for them, it is very important to be recognized and to have power. They will achieve excellence in any job where they will have the opportunity to develop these characteristics.

Financial managers, business owners, entrepreneurs, politicians, managers, CEOs, generals, and team captains.

The qualitative meaning of the Number 9

(Male, heart number, communicator)

Integrity and wisdom

Imagine an old castle. Now imagine a person walking down a hallway filled with closed doors. This person is very wise and brings a candle that gives light, for himself and for those who follow him. He knows which door to open and which one not to open. He knows where danger lurks and where it does not. Actually, he realizes that he is the only one to decide where to go.

If this story defines you, would you be able to get others to follow you?

Would you be a good example for others to follow?

Meaning of life

The way of those who have been bestowed with number 9 is to live in harmony with your own integrity and balance your life with the insight of the heart. The fact that you were born with a great charisma is evident because it is immediately recognized by others. As a number 9, you are a natural-born leader. Someone who effortlessly and, by the power of your natural charisma, leads others to follow you. The important thing you must understand is that, whether you do the right or wrong thing, others will follow you anyway. Whether you decide to lead a good or bad life, or a positive or negative existence, you should always remember that your behavior will affect others.

Strengths: Flexibility, humor, communication skills, linguistic talent, personality, reliability, intelligence, warmth, tolerance, patience, spirituality, sense of responsibility, joy of change, regeneration, truthfulness.

Points to ponder: superficiality, arrogance, chaos, bitterness, nervousness, competitiveness, guilt, hesitation, criticizes others and himself, intolerance, boredom, wanting to have fun.

Talents: Number 9's have a great disposition for communication and know how to lead others towards a certain goal. They are excellent as a managers, coaches, trainers and leaders. They make good lawyers and building contractors in construction. Those who are more sensitive become excellent psychologists or teachers, because they can easily empathize with people.

Management, coaching, trainers, leadership, contractors, lawyers, psychologists, teachers.

• • •

I am sure that after reading these few lines, you will never look at numbers in the same way as you may have once done.

A new world has opened up to you, and now nothing will be the same.

Now you have a new awareness that will help you to understand the best way to interpret numbers.

What you have learned thus far has nothing in common with the table of THE SECRET of NUMBERS. I only wanted to introduce you to the qualitative world of numbers, so you can begin to view them with a new set of eyes, even before you know the table.

• • •

The bad news

During many meetings and seminars, I have found that many people allow themselves to be influenced by external circumstances, circumstances that prevent them from dreaming or even wishing about having a new life.

Many people say they'd like to change jobs, move into a new house, or improve their emotional situation. But bad habits and routines are hard to break. They prevent them from taking action. Fear holds them back. Many are afraid to abandon the comfort zone of the status quo. In simple terms, they are afraid.

They are afraid of the new challenges they will face; they are afraid of what they might find once they leave the coast and find themselves out on the open sea.

Many people are stuck there. Many times, they will no longer allow their dreams to express themselves freely.

People naturally tend to move away from pain and move towards pleasure. Until the pain exceeds the pleasure, that person won't be compelled to change in his life.

But when their pain exceeds the pleasure, they must change. This is where they start moving in the direction of their new goal. Why am I telling you all this?

Because despite the information that you will discover from reading this book, on its own, it will do nothing to change your life unless you decide to embark on a new path. In fact, it's one thing to have a new understanding, yet quite another to apply it for the purpose of improving your life.

Now I want to tell you another secret: people can vibrate single numbers in a positive way, but they can also vibrate in a negative way without getting any of the benefits that come with it.

It will be up to you to decide how you want to vibrate. Your personal number has a great amount of energy. To understand the significance of the numbers, you will fill in the table to determine your chart with your SECRET of NUMBERS. Use this knowledge to make the move to a "higher level." Your chart represents a powerful map that will reveal to you the direction of your journey.

We need a new approach

Before reading the following pages, there are four important tips we must give you!

First – focus on what your intuition tells you. Pay attention to your feelings without listening to the doubts that will whisper in your mind.

Second – remember that there are judgments, or worse, prejudices about numbers, so put your focus and concentration on yourself and on YOUR own terms.

Third – as you prepare yourself to receive the message of THE SECRET of NUMBERS, take three deep breaths to free your energy, so you'll be ready for whatever the numbers want to send you.

Fourth – you must have "faith" that God wants to talk to you. So what exactly is faith? "Faith is the ability to see the invisible and believe in the incredible, and that is what enables believers to receive what the masses think is impossible."

Depend solely on your own intuition. Decide if you want to be a part of the believers or the masses.

• • •

You decide!

Who will approach the message of THE SECRET of NUMBERS with the desire to understand the deeper meaning of the words on the page, and be guided by them toward a change? If you choose to do it, you must always do it gradually, never abruptly. You will have the opportunity to learn about how to access your "higher level code." You may lay out a new route for yourself to follow, relying on unconditional faith. The ability to believe in the invisible, what you are still unable to see, touch, taste, or hold in the material world, in fact, is one of the most important skills for you to learn and develop in order to realize extraordinary things by using the table of THE SECRET of NUMBERS. For centuries, this knowledge has been handed down from hand to hand and used to assist humanity in its evolution. Now it will be up to you, depending on your current level of consciousness, to your sensitivity, to your desire to change, to your decisions, whether to receive the information, to interpret it and above all apply it in your life.

Since acquiring this new consciousness, I can confirm that my way of life has completely changed – in relation to my relationships, to the way I now communicate. When I am confronted with negative attitudes or strange reactions from people close to me, before getting angry, I analyze their table of THE SECRET of NUMBERS. The results make me smile, because their life number confirms for me that their reactions and attitudes are an unquestionable part of the characteristics of their personalities.

I realized that before they part ways, I would not have unnecessary discussions with them. Instead, I transformed our get-togethers back into laughter.

What's more beautiful than understanding their personalities and laughing instead?

Having had the opportunity to learn the meaning of numbers and understanding the interpretation that Monika has taught me has influenced all my relationships very positively.

Listening to what the table of THE SECRET of NUMBERS says will give the opportunity to make profound changes in your life that will allow you to fully express your true self.

Those who approach this in a skeptical way, or interpret this as a simple game to play with friends or family, may very well miss out on one of the most important occasions of their life. Perhaps they comprehend its power and they want to change, but imagine if they never implemented it to pursue their desires. What if they decided to put into practice the message of THE SECRET of NUMBERS, but they didn't take it as seriously as they should have? Most likely they would not get the benefits that could possibly allow them to achieve balance and inner harmony in their life. Or what if they spent the time pursuing it, but they never attained the results? What a shame all of those examples would be.

If you do not use this knowledge, you could again find yourself in uncomfortable situations, arguments, or quarrels. which unfortunately arise only because you're not applying the invisible side of the numbers as outlined herein.

You decide what is best for you: spending your days arguing and in a volatile state or hugging and smiling.

How did I figure it out?

Over the years, Monika has conducted thousands of consultations. And in every single reading, there's been a specific, individualized, and targeted message that the table of THE SECRET of NUMBERS informed her.

She has always received positive feedback, because all the people who have applied the chart of THE SECRET of NUMBERS have made remarkable improvements, from every point: professionally, physically, in the relationship of torque, and the relationship with their children. I'm one of them. After becoming more aware, through the knowledge of the meaning of the numbers of my birthday, I felt a great emotion inside, a deep sense of wonder and gratitude that the universe introduced me to this unique tool of extraordinary importance for everyday life.

The message of THE SECRET of NUMBERS has been a great challenge for me personally, because it was like standing naked in front of a large mirror. Initially, I focused on the wallpaper instead of looking deeply at myself. Eventually, I decided I wanted to get a firm grasp on the information. That's when I began to build a better relationship with myself. One based on trust and respect. I now understand it is no simple thing. Discovering all the basic features that characterize our personalities is a personal thing and takes a while to absorb.

But when I decided to put my all into understanding it, my life changed dramatically. My decision was one of not settling for just tiptoeing through life anymore, waking each day to an unhappy state of passive, daily resignation.

Beauty came when I decided to put the lessons into practice in my life. This meant I was finally serious about making major changes in my life.

As everyone knows, normally, people do not want to change, because they often carry around baggage from their past. It may be the unknown, or the feeling of not knowing where they're going, of losing the "certainties," or losing sight of their reference points that stops them in their tracks. Whatever it is that frightens them the most tends to scare them, blocking them from progress.

It was the same for me. When I decided to make profound changes to my life, I went through moments of great suffering, because I felt something inside of me would need to die forever to make room for the good I desired that wasn't even born yet.

And what happens to the caterpillar who suffers thinking he must die without knowing he is instead turning into a beautiful butterfly, who will rise and fly free from flower to flower? I admit that it was not an easy time in my life. But now I can say it was worth it!

I thought I would tell you about the history of numerology, but then I thought if you were so inclined to research it on your own, you could easily look it up on the Internet. Also, as I mentioned earlier, you could get a copy of Monika's first book, *1, 2, 3, Let's Talk About You!* There she discusses numerology in depth and gets to the heart of this wonderful science.

However, it's currently only available in Italian, which to many of the readers of this book may be an obstacle. So considering that I care a great deal about the fact that the information in this book will lead many of you to transform your lives, I'll spare you having to learn Italian just to read her first book. Everything you need to know is detailed here. Besides, you have direct access to us.

• • •

Our stories

Before diving into any more information, we thought we'd share a little bit about ourselves and our stories. I'll tell my story first, and then Monika will share hers.

Andrea Tonello

Birthdate – 03/31/1975
This is my story.

Italian tradition dictates the eldest son must take charge of the family business when he reaches adulthood. No matter what family he's born to, his life plan is predetermined for him. The vocation may be different, but the tradition remains the same. A farmer's son grows up to be a farmer; a cobbler's boy becomes a cobbler; or, as in my family's case, a barber's son must fulfill his destiny of cutting hair. Family tradition is so strong in my country that breaking out of the mold cast for you set down by the preceding generations is forbidden. In my childhood home in northern Italy's province of Vicenza, my family ardently clung to this idea. As a youngster, this never sat well with me, because it afforded me no opportunity to choose a future of my own. Early on, I decided to cast off these restrictions and choose my own path.

Lesson #1 – Make your own way in life.

The day my favorite elementary school teacher asked the class what we wanted to be when we grew up, without hesitation, I declared, "I want to be a lawyer." Perhaps it was my decisiveness or the defiant nature of my answer, but whatever it was, she encouraged me. "Bravo!" she said, clapping her hands. Learning of my ambition, my father dismissed it as a childhood fantasy since he'd been grooming me to be a barber all along. However, it wasn't a fantasy to me. **A small voice, like a soft breeze, had whispered to me**.

The day I decided to be a lawyer, the seed of that aspiration firmly planted itself in my mind. The idea took root, and the fantasy flashed pictures in my mind nonstop. In my waking hours, I daydreamed about how it would feel and what it would be like. At night, my dreams revealed a grown up me wearing suits and ties, arguing cases before a judge and jury, and celebrating with my clients after winning their cases in court. The idea excited my seven-year-old self, and the more I focused on it, the more it grew into a burning desire. From that young age, my life's mission became one of helping people to solve their legal problems.

As a teenager, the time had come for high school. My father became enraged when he learned of my plans to enroll. "Your grandfather is turning over in his grave!" he declared. "Your obligation is to your family, not to your own selfish wants. You must become a barber. School is unnecessary."

"I'm going to be an attorney," I said defiantly. Heated arguments erupted around the dinner table over plates of pasta. Everyone had an opinion about my future, and each did their part to change my mind. But I would hear nothing of their pleas, and instead, I held my ground. My determination was such that no amount of anger or pleading could dissuade me from pursuing my dream. Eventually, my father finally gave in, and I enrolled in high school. **The voice inside me cheered!**

Upon graduating from high school, once again, he attempted to assert his control over my future. "You've gotten very smart in the last five years," he said, attempting to approach me with calm emotion, "now you must run the barbershop." It felt like déjà vu. Why did he not respect my desire to pursue a future of my own choosing? Never being one to trade my happiness for the sake of keeping the family peace, I mustered all my courage and confronted him. "No!" I commanded adamantly. "It's too late. I've already enrolled in and paid tuition for law school. I'm going with or without your blessing." Any further arguments I dismissed with a flick of my wrist. His shoulders shrugged when he realized that he had been whipped. At long last, he gave up the fight and blessed me in the pursuit of my lifelong dream.

Lesson #2 – Hold fast to your dream, no matter what.

Looking back on that time, I realize now that being a barber would have made me miserable. I have nothing against barbers, we all need them, but I'd probably stab someone with scissors. Because I stood up to my father and fought for myself, I passed through an invisible barrier from boyhood to stand on the other side as a powerful man. A new understanding of my own power began to emerge from this rite of passage. Self-determination and self-direction were two important traits I acquired all those years ago when I stuck up for myself. More importantly, the realization that having a dream and making the decision to keep it alive over a sustained period of time served me well to bring my goal into reality.

After law school, I received an apprenticeship as a civil servant in Italy's National Archives. My first assignment was to move the library's contents from its original location to a new home. For 12 months, I removed books from their shelves and wiped them clean before boxing them up and transferring them to a villa of extraordinary beauty. The hours were long and tedious, but I didn't mind. In fact, just being in the presence of those books inspired me. Oftentimes, I'd leaf through pages and read the writings of classical authors such as Seneca and Marcus Aurelius as well as those of contemporary writers. Their teachings on philosophy, life, love, happiness, and an individual's life purpose stirred something deep in me. I experienced the beginnings of an awakening. Was I truly living up to my fullest potential? I'd take these books home and read them into the wee hours, pondering their ancient wisdom. **There was that voice in my head again, but what was it saying?**

My good fortune continued when the owner of a private law firm in Vicenza saw potential in me and gave me my first real job even though I hadn't yet completed my law school course work. Of course, I had to balance my workload with my school, but eventually, I graduated and passed the bar. All I could think about was how grateful I felt for having finally achieved my dream.

My job at the law firm continued once I was a full-fledged attorney, and the owner relied on me more and more. One day, when he was running late, he asked me to take his place in an appointment, and I agreed. The moment the client, Michela, walked into the office, I fell madly in love with her. The way she reached out her hand to shake mine, the beautiful smile she flashed me when she introduced herself, and the radiance of her skin shone when the light caught it just so captivated me. Sparks flew between us, and we soon began dating. Eventually, we married.

For the next few years, life progressed in an upward spiral, each milestone surpassing the last. By the age of 34, I had built my own financially successful law firm, married the love of my life, and welcomed our daughter, Arianna, into the world. Despite having what appeared to be a perfect life, a feeling of discontent crept into my subconscious, zapping joy from my life. The time had come to look beyond my original dream and find a new one. But where should I start? Introspection provided me with the answer I sought – find happiness and deeper meaning in life. I reflected on the time when I was the happiest in my life. **The voice inside yelled too loudly for me to ignore any longer.**

Lesson #3 – Recreate yourself when the compulsion seizes you.

My mind returned to the happiness I felt turning the pages of those old books, mulling over their teachings, and reflecting on their wisdom. Seeking answers to life's bigger questions was the most fulfilling period in my life. A rekindled zest for life seized me, fanning a flame within me to pursue this kind of knowledge again. Curiosity led me to discover modern day thought leaders such as Bob Proctor, Deepak Chopra, and the Dalai Lama, among others. These teachers had wisdom and were still alive. I bought their books and devoured them, highlighting, underlining and rereading every chapter. I made it my goal to have them as mentors.

Before stumbling upon these teachings, I had never heard the term "Personal Development," even though I had been unconsciously practicing it for years. Until that point, I had strived with a dogged determination to create a successful life by putting all my effort on my external environment. I had been focused on the visible world outside of myself. However, the advice of these teachers directed me to turn my focus inward to the invisible side of myself, the universe of thought and spirit, heretofore unexplored consciously. Now, I had the means to identify things that I had only previously had a feeling about, although I always knew they were there. Pieces to a puzzle began falling into place. **"Pay attention," the voice said**.

Lesson #4 – Seek the help of mentors.

The next phase of my journey took me to transformational seminars where I met like-minded people all interested in personal growth. At one particular event in Milan, a woman took the stage and spoke of a method of reading numbers of people's birthdates and interpreting them by means of an ancient process. Her name was Monika Ben Thabetova. So impressed, I found her in the lobby during a break and asked to speak to her further about her numbers system. Unfortunately, there wasn't enough time at the seminar to meet, but she agreed to schedule a Skype call in the coming days. During our session, she read the significance of my birthdate numbers, telling me things about myself no one else knew. She told me I was a teacher, and my destiny was to write books and become a motivational speaker. "You know this is true if you'd tune into the voice inside." This took me by surprise. How did she know about that voice? Her words rang true and gave me a new perspective on my life's mission, but how would I move forward?

I asked for Monika's help. If I were to walk a new spiritual path, I would need assistance; and she agreed to help me. Once a month, we hiked majestic mountain trails above Lake Como and talked about life and our destinies. Over time, she pulled back the veil that shrouded the secret of numbers and their special energy. I began to study and understand the amazing power of this tool. "Everything is a number," she explained, "and each has its own significance in our lives that is beyond our comprehension." In a flash, the voice echoed in my head, telling me to bring the secret of numbers to the world. When I told her about it, she nodded knowingly. "We are meant to work together."

A new meaning for my life emerged, but to get the word out on a grand scale, I would need to enlist the help of people who had a global following. Before I had begun to study personal development material, I would have been paralyzed at not knowing how. But now I knew as long as I had a clear vision of my goal, the way would be shown.

During an online class hosted by Bob Proctor, he had a guest, *New York Times* best-selling author, Peggy McColl, who I somehow knew would play a role in helping us launch THE SECRET of NUMBERS. Her specialty is coaching people to launch their books, make them best-sellers, and build businesses around their concepts.

Currently, Monika and I are working to bring our book, online classes, and live seminars to life with the help of Bob & Peggy. These two mentors are beacons of hope transmitting a message that anyone can change the world if they can dream it up and have the guts to bring it into reality.

Since embarking on my new mission, the voice in my head has gone silent. It isn't as though it's gone away or left my head, but rather, since my life's purpose and my intuition are now in alignment, I believe the two voices have merged as one.

In conclusion, my story wouldn't be complete without thanking my wife, my daughter, and our dog for embracing my desire to be more, and to Monika, who has entrusted me to nurture her dream as if it were my own. Of course, I must thank my father, the barber, without whom I never would've had the courage to dare to grow into the man that I am today.

Monika Ben Thabetova

Birthdate – 05/30/1976

This is my story.

The idea may have crept into your mind to wonder how on earth I ever became interested in numbers and the science of numerology in the first place. It also may have crossed your mind to wonder how I ever got the idea that numbers were trying to get me to transmit their important messages through me for the sake of mankind. In my first book, I told my story. Now, I will do my best to give a more thorough version with added nuances as well as a few more thrills.

"And why is this?" you ask curiously. I definitely don't want to sound like someone who feels sorry for herself or who plays the victim role in life because of certain tragedies or circumstances that have befallen me. Alternatively, I'd like to motivate you through my personal story. My wish is that my life experience persuades you to get up off the couch or dry your tears, look to the sky with gratitude, and, with a smile, take on adventures that life has prepared especially for you.

Before you immerse yourself in my story, I'd like you to know about my personal mission to help people increase their self-awareness while understanding themselves and others better. During my journey over the past several years as a teacher, I have met so many people who have shared their incredible stories with me. There have been too many to count. Everyone is living their life, and yet the greatest miracle is that nobody is experiencing the same narrative. Never have I encountered two life stories that were exactly the same, nor have I ever met two people who were exactly alike. Each story is as unique as the person who lives it. By this I mean to express that my story is one among many but altogether unique.

I was born on 05/30/1976 in Brno, the Czech Republic to a Czech mother and african father – a mixed marriage, which was very unusual at the time in the then-Communist country.

As a toddler, my parents moved me to Africa a large village in the middle of the desert. Playing with other children in a cotton field surrounded by farm animals and village women comprise my earliest memories. I also remember feeling lonely because my older brother had stayed behind with our grandmother since he'd already started school. From my mother's recollections, I've gathered that in the center of the village stood a great chieftain's tent.

Every evening, he would gather the villagers to entertain them with his mystical stories. I remember sitting in the dust, playing with pebbles like a typical toddler, unaware of the lessons this shaman taught with his words. One day before returning to Europe, my mom was called to his tent where, in a trance-like state, he whispered in her ear, "You'll never have to worry about your daughter. She is a special child. For she will lead an exciting and eventful life."

One year later, infected with yellow fever and weak from malaria, my mother and I fled my father, and retreated to the safety of Czechoslovakia, never to return to Africa again.

At five, my identity shifted from Muna Mirghani Monika Mirghaniova to Monika Sera when my mother's new husband adopted me. We left the big city of Brno for the quiet life in Lysice, a village of a thousand souls. Here's where my vivid memories started, and they weren't happy.

My problems began in kindergarten. Ignorance, intolerance, and communism are to blame. As a girl with dark skin and kinky hair, I was an outsider, a foreigner. Perhaps villagers had seen someone like me in magazines or on television. But with the pervasive communistic censorship, people had limited views. In any case, other children were forbidden from playing with me because I was different, strange. I was the only black egg in a nest of white ones. I shed many tears on my mother's lap after returning home from school. In elementary school, the situation worsened. Nobody wanted to sit next to me; no one wanted to touch me; not a single person wanted to play with me. They were afraid of getting dirty. Unfortunately, the teachers were complicit, isolating me on a secluded bench in a corner at the back of the classroom. And I slowly retreated inward, taking refuge in a world of fantasies and dreams. Dreams of a seven-year-old girl.

It soon became apparent that my new father had serious alcohol problems. When he drank, he became a monster. I was forced to watch horrific scenes of violence visited upon my mother. Sometimes, I wonder how I was able to manage watching such brutality.

Meanwhile, school got worse. My classmates made fun of me, telling me I'd been abandoned and left under a bush, explaining my adoption. Doubt crept in as I even started to wonder if my mother was even my real mother. All this because I was dark complectioned while my mother was fair. Support was non-existent, even from my teachers. During a lesson on prehistoric man, I was called to the front of the class to show how my profile resembled that of a Neanderthal, making the classroom erupt in laughter. Despite excelling in athletics, beating all the challengers in running and jumping, I was never allowed to represent my school in competitions because of my skin color. Prejudice was common during this period.

One day, my mother was aghast to see my bloody knees when I returned home. During physical education class, my instructor dragged me into the shower and scrubbed the skin from my knees in an attempt to "clean" away my pigment. My mother's angry visit to the school didn't help matters, because afterward, I was treated even worse than before.

After school, my loneliness and isolation disappeared during long walks in the woods with Rexa, my only friend, who listened to my every stories of humiliation, licking away the tears. This dog was the best gift my mother had ever given to me. During summer break, Rexa and I roamed the woods, picking wild strawberries, cherries, mushrooms, and blackberries. In winter, my hikes became even more pleasurable because I was able to track paw prints of wild animals in the snow. Without judgment, nature's respite welcomed me during the challenges of my upbringing.

My mother's responsibility to her children caused her to work long hours. Oftentimes, she'd have to pick up extra shifts to cover the lost earnings of my drunk father, who frequently missed work due to drunkenness. To pick up the slack, my grandmother babysat my brother and me every weekend. Her positive influence exposed me to the theater, art museums, and the symphony. She sewed me nice clothes, telling wonderful fairy tales as she pulled the needle through the fabric. But she also had a negative side. Instead of combing my curly hair, she'd tease it into a knotted mess. "Your hair is impossible!" she'd exclaim before throwing up her arms in surrender. Her encouragement in my singing, dancing or especially walking was lacking. "You walk like a duck and will never get a husband if we don't correct it," she'd spew, sending me to her room to walk for hours on the straight edge of a rug, away from the excitement my brothers and cousins were watching on the television set.

My little sister came along when I was nine. She became my surrogate doll whom I doted on, played with, and cared for after school. After another of his violent rants, my father entered a detox center. I stayed home and cared for my little sister while my mother occupied herself with my father's care. Upon his return, life became almost pleasant for several years until at 14 when my new-found self-awareness brought on a slew of questions. "Why is my skin so dark?" "Where is my birth father?" "Why do you always change the channel when there's a black athlete on television?" "Why can't we talk about Africa at home?" I bombarded my mother and grandmother with questions. They were close-lipped about anything regarding my past. In secret, I began researching my origins. My brother and I sent letter after letter to various embassies around the world, never receiving a response. One day, I found a photograph of a black man stuck between the pages of an old book in my grandmother's house. Based on the likeness, I could tell it was my father. From that moment on, I always kept it with me. Teenage fantasies of my father filled my head. The decision was made – No matter what, I will go to the ends of the earth to find him. Nearly three years of searching – numerous calls and letters to various Arabic embassies – proved fruitful. One day, my grandmother's phone rang, and it was HIM! My heart overflowed with happiness to hear his voice. Although we could barely communicate, because he was speaking Arabic and me Czech. But in a broken English, he promised to come for a visit, and my heart soared. Unfortunately, when he said, "I am coming next week," he didn't mean it. Time after time, he either missed his flight or his meeting went too long. Whatever excuse he could fabricate, he did. Every phone call and every missed meeting left me feeling disappointed.

Locked in my room and feeling depressed, I assuaged my loneliness by drawing black scribbles on white paper. From the kitchen, my mother cried out, "Come here, I want to teach you something very important." After no response, she beckoned again, "It'll change your life."

By no means did I want to hear the usual parental pep talk. But there was a sincerity in her voice that piqued my curiosity enough to get up off my bed and join her at the kitchen table. With pen in hand, she began to draw out a series of lines, creating a graph. Then she handed me the pen and said, "Write down your birthdate."

"Why don't you do it? Did you forget my birthday?" I asked her with sarcastic teenage incredulity.

"Just write it," she said.

Reluctantly, I grabbed the pen and jotted it down. She pointed at the various boxes and explained its meaning. After about 10 minutes, I looked at her wide-eyed and said, "The numbers have a special energy, and they can give us valuable information about anything and anyone. Yeah, right. Whatever, Mom." I gave her a kiss on the forehead, stuffing the folded sheet of paper into my pocket, and returned to my room.

Thus began my introduction to the world of numbers. For a long time, the piece of paper with the table filled in sat in the drawer of my nightstand, collecting dust. Occasionally, I'd pick it up and look at the numbers before dropping back in its place before closing it back inside the drawer. For some unknown reason, I was strangely drawn to this piece of paper.

Two years had passed before I approached her again about the table. "How did you find out about the birthdates?" I asked.

"In 1968, I saw a magazine article about the energy of numbers with the table and a short explanation. I tore it out and tucked it away in the library for safe keeping, thinking I'd figure out how to use it later. It wasn't until 20 years later, while packing to move to the new house, that it flew out of a faded magazine. When I picked it up off the floor, I remembered it immediately. With great effort, I deciphered what was still visible of the explanation of the table, and then I memorized it. I now realize that the numbers in the table are a tool, a method, something special."

It was at this point that I started to pay closer attention to the numbers on the piece of paper stuffed away in my nightstand drawer.

My teenage years suddenly improved the day I found my first two real friends. They loved me even though their mothers forbade the association. Having friends changed my outlook on life in a positive way. We soon began to spend as much time together as we could. Shortly thereafter, my mother enrolled me in a high school located 10 km away, forcing me to take the bus every day and spending less time with my new friends. I found the study of Agronomy and Animal Husbandry interesting, but once again the color of my skin posed a problem. It didn't present itself until my second year. According to the administration, I spoiled the school's reputation. As a way to restore the school's good name, a plot was organized for my removal. In the middle of my Chemistry class, the director entered the room, accompanied by police, to accuse me of stealing the belongings of other students. I was transported to the police station where I was told, "If you confess to the charges brought against you, we won't expel you from school. And we won't tell your parents." Terrified and trembling, I did as I was told, admitting to everything even though I didn't know what the authorities were talking about. The next morning, I returned to school just like any other day except that five hours later, I was handed a letter of exclusion. Standing there motionless and in shock, I thought about how they had all lied to me. Unsure about what to do or where to go, I eventually decided to head home.

"What are you doing home so early?" my mother asked.

"I was expelled," I confessed, falling into her loving arms like a blubbering fool. After I explained the entire situation to her, she became angry with the school officials as well as the police. "How could they do such an unjust thing to my little girl?" she raged. So began yet another battle with the Czech school system.

Between the court hearings examining my case against the school, we searched far and wide for a new school. Obviously, no school in our province wanted a hoodlum like me as one of their students. After great research, we finally found a school which at the time was studying Angolan culture. As a result of an agreement reached with the state of Czechoslovakia, I was allowed to enroll. Finally, my skin color was no longer an issue. The only problem was that the school was located 200 km from my house or a 3-hour bus ride. Twice a day, I rode the bus to my new school to continue my studies. Every morning, I was up at 4:30 a.m. and, at times, I wasn't back home until eleven o'clock at night. This took a toll on me, but I was determined to finish school.

A year of hearings on my case brought good news. All charges were dropped when it was discovered that I hadn't stolen anything. Every part of the story had been fabricated to have me expelled from school. Instead of filing a racial discrimination suit against the institution, my mother and I decided we were happy for the acquittal. The truth had come out, and we had no desire to continue to associate with those types of people.

At my new school, many things changed for the better. Because neither the teachers nor the other students were yet accustomed to seeing people of color, I was placed into a classroom of all white students. Nobody teased me. Nobody made fun of me. Nobody made me feel bad about being me. For the greater part of 16 years, I had been tormented because of the way I looked, so this new found acceptance gave me a new lease on life.

After the first year of school, I fell in love – a totally new experience for me. Then at 17, I got pregnant – also a new experience for me.

During the fifth month of my pregnancy, the father of my child disappeared, which hurt me deeply. It was a suffering only understood by someone who has experienced an equivalent loss. I gave birth to a healthy baby girl, but because of the responsibilities that come with motherhood, I took a year off from my education.

At that time, my mother and I were very close, and my stepfather was clean and sober, so I was able to resume my studies. Every morning, I continued to wake up at half past four to prepare everything for the baby. Then I went to school. In the evenings, I'd wash, iron, cook and do all the things that a single mother raising a child alone would do.

When did I find the time to study? On the bus, of course! Clocking 400 km a day inside a bus gave me enough time to do my homework. I even prepared for my final exams on that bus.

When my daughter was nine months, and after I had earned my bachelor's degree, fate put a man in my path, who a year and a half later would become my husband.

Six months after the wedding, our first marital problems appeared, followed by a few misunderstandings, which led to the first in-depth discussion I'd ever had with another person about my past. I finally understood why I constantly asked, "Why me? Why me?" Being a victim was my MO. In detailing the trauma of my childhood and my teenage years, the conversation with my husband explained the pain I was dealing with. I was living through the effects of Post Traumatic Stress Disorder.

One day, while straightening up my bedside table, I picked up the piece of paper with my birthdate on it. I felt an inexplicable respect for it. I treated that "piece of paper" as if it were the most important thing in my life.

At 21, my health rapidly deteriorated. I began to have serious problems with my kidneys, intestines, and my entire urinary system. A continuous recurrence of facial paralysis, problems with the nervous system, chronic sore throats, and weight gain alarmed my family and me. The doctor prescribed many medicines: cortisone, diuretics, and antibiotics. And when they didn't work, he admitted me to the hospital with symptoms of bloating, depression, and manic emotional swings. I felt so hopeless that I couldn't even bring myself to smile. I saw only darkness in the world.

While lying alone in my hospital bed, an inner voice cried out, "It's time!"

"Time for what" I queried.

"It's time for you to take responsibility for your life and your health. It's time for you to stop blaming others for your conditions. Don't take refuge in the disease; it's time to stop being a victim. It's time you stopped feeling sorry for yourself. Childhood and adolescence are not easy for anyone. Grow up now, Monika. You're a mother now!" the voice scolded.

I decided that the voice was right! It was time. It was time to get better and smile again for my daughter, for my husband, but mostly for myself.

Suddenly, the question of "How should I do it?" popped into my head. From nowhere came the answer, **"Everything you need to know about yourself and your loved ones can be found in the numbers of your birthdates. Everything you will need to come back and be happy is found in the numbers. It's time to help others and to regain your smile."** The desire to find a piece of paper and a pen overtook me. All at once, I began to write the birthdates of everyone I knew. I built their tables, read their numbers and listened to what the numbers had to tell me about every single person. A nurse checked in on me and was frightened by my sudden boost of energy. She immediately called a doctor. It must've looked like I was a madwoman. In the span of a few minutes, I'd scattered the completed charts of a dozen people on my bed, on my table and even on the floor.

At that moment, in a hospital bed, with an IV sticking out of my arm, overweight and under the influence of various types of drugs, I finally understood how to interpret the subtle vibration of numbers. I really and truly felt it. Right then I did not know what to do! I wanted to shout to the whole world, but I was locked in a hospital room... I remember that night I rolled my IV unit to the window to look at the sky, and with tears in my eyes, I took in the enormity of the vast night. While watching the stars, the only thing I could think to say was, "Thank you. Thank you. Thank you."

When I arrived home from the hospital, my perspective on life had changed. The way I felt was different too. Not only because of the color of my skin and my curly hair but how I felt inside. Of course, this was nothing I ever felt I could share with my mother; she wouldn't have understood. In the meantime, I continued calculating the birthdates of famous people, neighbors, athletes, my husband's friends, and virtually anyone in my life. It was inexplicable to me that I understood how to plunge so deeply into another person's psyche.

Obviously, my story does not end at the age of 22. Because I'd endured such terrible racial attacks and other humiliations in my country during my youth, I was forced to face the facts as an adult. My husband, my daughter, and I felt compelled to seek freedom elsewhere to escape the oppression in the Czech Republic. We chose to settle in Italy. I've had the good fortune of expanding my understanding of numbers in the safety of a Democratic country that values individual freedom.

• • •

Chapter 2

THE CHART of THE SECRET of NUMBERS

With great deference and respect, it's now time to approach the much-touted table of THE SECRET of NUMBERS that we've mentioned throughout our book so far.

Get ready because you're about to learn a secret that will change your life!

Since the dawn of civilization, the ancient peoples have always used various systems of calculating and interpreting numbers to assist in living better lives, to forecast the weather, or to determine the best time for planting crops. However, I have discovered a unique system of reading the hidden meaning behind the numbers you see every day.

You'll discover things that will make you happy, but others you'll have great trouble accepting. Maybe you may not resonate with some of the information. Or perhaps you'll be angered by the revelations. The madder you become, the deeper what is revealed will affect you. It'll just be confirmation that some part of what you are doing in your life will need work. At times, you may even feel like closing the book and tossing it aside as invalid, because you don't like what the numbers reveal. It's right at that moment I am going encourage you to hang on. Don't close the book. Instead, continue reading. Ask yourself (and be honest) whether the revelation about yourself has validity. Begin to question yourself. It is imperative that you do this soul searching in a quiet place and when you are alone ... alone with yourself. I am not asking for perfection here, just tiny steps for self-reflection, self-awareness, and self-improvement. In order to evolve and to live your life more harmoniously, you'll need to retreat into your true inner world where only you hear the conversations. Become mindful.

And what is mindfulness?

Many books claim it's what we think, say, and how we act. This is true. But it goes much deeper than that. True mindfulness is the awareness, the consciousness that precedes thought.

Yes, I repeat once again: it is consciousness that precedes thought...

Are you ready to go on a transformational journey?

Are you ready to get a deeper understanding of yourself?

Are you ready for the knowledge of a thought so deep that it gives you a completely different perception of yourself? A whole new consciousness? A brand new awareness?

Perfect.

Then grab a piece of paper and a pen, and let's begin.

The table of THE SECRET of NUMBERS consists of 4 rows and 4 columns.

The easiest thing to do is draw a rectangle and divide it into 16 squares.

So each number has its own place within its own box.

Let me quickly answer the question that crosses people's minds – Are two people born on the same day, month and year equal?

The answer – No! Every one of us is different, special, and unique. No two people are ever exactly alike. We're all born with strengths and weaknesses that are different from those of anyone else. I will never understand how it is possible that two people can attend the same class with the same teacher, but get different results. True understanding of the power of our table comes at the point that we recognize each individual's own unique diversity.

When two people share the same birthdate, we must always take into account that nobody is born into the same family, in the same city, in the same state, with the same religion, the same company, and in the same circumstances. Each of which has a strong influence on our external environment. I give you an extreme example: imagine a child is born in a poor African country. At three years of age, he fights for survival walking barefoot in a torn shirt, sleeping on the street, begging for food. He is alone in the world without a father or a mother to care for him. When he is six years old, he finds work wherein he toils, scrimps, and saves his money so that at 20, he may have the opportunity to emigrate.

Suppose instead that on the other side of the world, in the West, the same day, the same month, and the same year, a child is born to a wealthy family. At three years of age, he'll still be coddled by his mother. At six, he will start school, sleeping every night in his own bed in his own room. There will be so many games and clean clothes that he won't ever have time to use them all. He will be loved by his family and live without worries. At 20, his parents will give him the keys to a car they bought for him, just in time for him to drive to college.

In your opinion, do you think these two boys who were born on the same day, the same month, and the same year will lead the same lives? Never! It's impossible because they may have characteristics dictated by their date of births, but their individual circumstances that shaped them.

Their dates of birth tell us, for example, that they're both strong and expansive thinkers capable of making good decisions. But perhaps the boy from the West was raised by overprotective parents who made every decision for him, from which school to attend, which sports to play to which clothes to wear. In this case, when he grows up, he will most likely suffer greatly with his decision-making abilities, cultivating relationships with people who will make his decisions for him. Later on, expressing what he wants could become a problem because of the constant control his parents imposed on him as a child. At some point in adulthood, he could also need the guidance of a therapist to resolve his fear of making decisions or his fear of failure.

And what about the little African boy? When he grows up, he will probably be confronted with an opposite set of problems. Becoming combative, aggressive, thinking that it's necessary to fight for everything in life may plague him. Being a team player may be an issue for him because he's never needed to cooperate with others. Submitting to the rules may also be hard for him as he'll be used to having the final say in the discussions. As an adult, he could experience legal problems with the justice system and possibly face jail time.

And to think, both boys were born on the same day, month, and year.

Twins won't even be exactly the same. Each of them will confront difficult situations that differ from that of the other. One may be the favorite while the other may act out in an attempt to get attention. Oftentimes, twins are the complete opposite of their sibling. I hope I have adequately responded to a question that I've been asked more than any other during my twenty-year career as a numerologist.

One last thing before diving into the table of THE SECRET of NUMBERS. I thought I'd share a few of my client's stories.

Diego Gioia

As a catering director, I deal with business development and staff training.

Growing up, my family was very close. My parents loved us deeply, but they also punished us severely. This treatment led me to be judgmental toward myself and others. I was always a quiet child, withdrawn and closed, who preferred being alone, never truly capable of establishing real bonds with others. At 15, I became rebellious because of my inability to accept my homosexuality. For six years, I battled with my parents for fear of them not accepting me. When I turned 21, I came out to them, and to my surprise, they handled it beautifully! From that point forward, our relationship blossomed.

In truth, I was never happy with myself, so I took refuge in my studies and in my work. My self-loathing took on a life of its own, preventing me from even looking at myself in the mirror. My world consisted of a thousand anxieties and fears, which caused me to feel increasingly inadequate in any situation. I didn't understand the concept of good self-esteem; I only liked myself if someone else liked me first. The only things of importance were my ideas, principles, morals. and beliefs. Being as judgmental as I was, I had a scorched earth policy when it came to friends – they were either with me or against me. My moods alternated from periods of extreme calm to bursts of aggression that destroyed my relationships.

In 2012, I left a job that everyone envied, deciding I could no longer live in perpetual war with the world. I knew I had to make some personal changes. At dinner one evening during my sabbatical year, my mother asked if I'd like to accompany her to a numerology conference given by a woman named Monika. Very curious to learn about the science of numbers, I agreed. As the most skeptical person in the room that evening, I bombarded Monika with a thousand questions. By the end, still not content, I scheduled an appointment with her for the next day. As soon as I sat down with Monika at our appointment, she said, "Diego, first of all, I'm not here to judge you. Neither will I tell you only the good things about you, because you already know them. Instead, I'll tell you everything that blocks your awareness and what you need to work on to improve yourself and your life." That put me at ease right away. From that moment on, I began my journey with her, feeling privileged to have met her. With the precision of a surgeon and the grace of an angel, she dug deep into my soul, releasing monstrous thoughts and words. She uncovered things I had never uttered to anyone – not my parents, not my brother, not my friends, not even to my partner. After all, I had never admitted them to myself.

I was given the keys to unlock a profound personal understanding, not immediately evident. Clarity arrived like a fog lifting from a sunny day. Better still, I gained an understanding of who I was and what I wanted to do, have, and become. People who thought they knew me suddenly didn't recognize me. Until this point, I didn't even know what love was. How could I love someone else if I didn't even know how it felt to love myself?

My guardian angel, Monika, accompanied me as I embarked on this new life path. Problems I encountered that would have previously destroyed me became just new things to solve. Because in life, everything is eventually resolved. I learned to live in the present, to give myself no expectations, to release resentment, and to thank those who have hurt me.

I no longer judge, nor do I hate. Now I just focus on the mission that having the awareness of having a quiet love in my heart can really accomplish miracles. I like to breathe life into people, leaving them with a feeling of enrichment when we part. Looking at issues from every perspective allows me the freedom to not be afraid. Living with a spirit of spontaneity puts a smile my face. It's healthy to give away pieces of ourselves like breadcrumbs on the ground, a track that at the end of our lives will lead us back to us.

And most essentially, we must be AWARE OF OUR LIFE, because only then can we play our role on the stage of life. Otherwise, we run around like ants in an anthill like good little soldiers, making little progress toward self-evolution in the end.

From the start, Monika entered my DNA, guiding me to find a part of myself that I didn't even know I had. I am now a happy man, living intensely every day to spread joy for myself and those around me. With all the problems and challenges that life hands all of us, at least I now know where I'm going. I wonder where I would be if I had stayed in my comfort zone?

It is with gratitude to life that I now know the endless possibilities that the science of numbers has given me. With my newfound awareness, my brain can only think of ways that I can improve myself.

One might say that we are born only when we have become aware.

I dedicate my experience to Monika and to her science of numbers. A fine mind that with nine numbers can explain things better than a thousand teachers.

Luciano and Luisa Marai

These lines are few, but they have great value, telling you about the change in our lives since we met Monika and Andrea.

We've been a couple for many years, both sharing similar values and knowing the difference between right and wrong.

As people, our lives were a series of happy and sad moments. Luciano thrived in a job from which he received great satisfaction. Every day, I gave the best of myself, which rewarded me with great financial success. But this came at a cost; long business trips abroad kept me away from my family for long periods.

One evening in the summer of 2011, as usual, I was at work after recently returning from a business trip. Like every other night when I wasn't traveling, I drove my scooter. But this night was different. It ended in a serious accident.

Suddenly, I was back to being a child, unable to do anything on my own. After months in the intensive care unit, I was finally released to go home. Unfortunately, the burden of caring for me fell upon my wife and my son, for whom I'd always had great affection. At home, the same few questions swam through my mind repeatedly like fish in a fishbowl. What's the point of all this? Why did this happen to me? and Why all this pain? Years passed, and the hospital became my second home. It was time for me to make some changes. I decided to seek out answers to these questions that had plagued me for years.

On February 15, 2016, an advertisement for a series of community events circulated in our city. My wife suggested we attend a conference on numerology, something totally unknown to us.

Not sure what to expect, we arrived to find the hall full of people. I found a quiet corner out of public view. A beautiful woman took the stage and began her talk about numbers. At one point, she addressed me. "The gentleman with the blue jacket who is sitting in the back, please give me your birthdate." Although I was a bit embarrassed that she picked me out, I gave it to her. Without hesitation, she drew out a chart and began to calculate my numbers. My initial reaction was to think that what she was doing was insignificant, unimportant. That is until she started telling me the meaning of the numbers. Shocked and amazed, I just sat there in a daze as she identified all my issues. Her interpretation of my numbers answered every question I'd been asking myself since the accident.

At the conclusion of the conference, we waited several hours for the chance to talk to Monika and Andrea. There were so many people there who were hungry for this information. When we finally got our chance, Monika welcomed us warmly with her gorgeous smile. In short order, she'd jotted down our birthdates and talked us through the table that she'd drawn and filled in, making us understand many things about ourselves. Before leaving, we scheduled a Skype appointment for our whole family.

Thanks to Monika's numbers system and chart, she was able to explain to each of us exactly why situations and events had happened in our lives. She identified individual characteristics, both critical and affirmative, weaknesses, and strengths in each of us, advising us how best to resolve various situations. She taught us to deliberately look beyond appearances, conditions, circumstances, and people with awareness and intention. In essence, she gave us the key to understanding our lives!

Since that time, everything has changed for the better. Once we implemented her methodologies, a true comprehension of how numbers play a part in our lives emerged, and the appropriate corresponding actions and responses organized themselves for different, and more importantly, better outcomes in every facet of our lives.

Now we attend every numerology course Monika and Andrea offer. Our circle of friends has changed to a set of more positive and sincere people, who all want to improve themselves and the lives of the people around them.

We thank Monika, who taught us how to make important life changes to reap the best experience possible.

Our testimony is an invitation to anyone who needs to change their lives and understand themselves better. Turn to Monika – she's a special person, a true professional who, in a very honest and loving way, sometimes tells you what can at times be hard to hear. But if you listen to her, you will benefit greatly.

And, finally, on a personal note, we'd like to say a great big THANK YOU to Monika and Andrea for the wealth of knowledge and the freedom you have given us.

Manuela De Simone Esculapio

My athletic career began at the age of eight when I entered my first ice skating competition. I loved every part of competing: training, learning new skills, and strengthening my body. The pinnacle of my career brought me to the top of the national scene. Unfortunately, due to an accident that resulted in an injury to my hip and pelvis, my blossoming career ended, forcing me to retire well before reaching my potential. I sank into a depression and felt like a failure. Little did I know how important this break from the rigors of athletic training would be, because after I had fully recovered from my injury, a door opened to what was to be my true life path and career.

At the age of 14, I picked up my first barbell. It set me on a course that immersed my mind and body into the fitness world. It had taken several years before my vision was fully formed, but in 2014, an opportunity presented itself to enter the world of competitive bodybuilding. It was a sign that I latched onto. Suddenly, the vision had me, and it wouldn't let me go. In quick succession, I entered and won my first two competitions, qualifying for World Championships in Miami. Everything happened quickly as my vision crystallized before my very eyes. A little voice inside of me whispered, "Enter the IFBB federation competition, and one day you could win the Miss Olympia title or even the prestigious Arnold Classic!"

Bodybuilding became my obsession. I embraced the discipline and total focus as my reason for living, reducing my social life to zero. Daily workouts were grueling, and my diet required enormous sacrifices and hardships – a total year-long commitment. Sports at this high level are not for everyone; I understand that. In fact, it's a lifestyle that you must be married to. I have always been a warrior, ready for the necessary sacrifices to reach my goal. Problems surfaced as soon as I decided to take the most decisive step of my career – to enter the prestigious IFBB federation competition.

So my dark period of frustration, weariness, depression, isolation and solitude began. Friends and family withdrew their support, unable to understand my new lifestyle. They soon dropped off the radar which was fine by me as I had little energy to give outside the gym. My workouts were my focus. Big changes started happening to my body as with my mind. The psychological pressure became oppressive. One day, when I was on the verge of quitting, one of my few remaining friends called me concerned. She said, "There's a person named Monika Ben Thabetova who can help you." At the time, I didn't realize this woman would change my life.

As a natural skeptic, I did not believe she could help me, so I didn't reach out to her right away. Several months had passed before I felt compelled to contact her. During our first Skype meeting, we immediately connected. She scribbled down some numbers on a piece of paper and then she read them to me. It felt as though she was flipping through my life. It was very impressive. The things she said cracked open a hole in my head and heart, and shed light where only darkness had been. I had clarity again. She became my life coach, supporting me along my difficult path. Under her guidance, I've achieved goals I never imagined possible. I won my first competition in the IFBB, the prestigious Farnese Hercules Trophy, and I qualified to represent Italy in the Miss Olympia competition, a lifelong dream.

In my first attempt, I made it all the way to the semifinals, placing me ahead of other athletes who were more experienced than me at the international level.

Monika has taught me to visualize my success, to believe in my potential, and to leverage my solitude to my advantage. Even today, I still rely on her teachings and support to view every challenge as an opportunity for growth. I know I will reach my goals because I now believe in myself. Determination and persistence are my greatest assets. The advice I give anyone reading this is to never give up. Don't let yourself quit at the first sign of difficulties, because that is precisely when we're given the greatest opportunity to prove our worth. If you do this, nothing thereafter will ever be the same. You will excel at whatever you put your mind to, because the universe conspires in our favor; it must since it brought Monika into my life.

Monika, you're an extraordinary woman to whom I can only say thank you, from the bottom of my heart.

Mauro Ferraro

I own a small accounting firm of 200 employees in the province of Vicenza, located in the northeastern Italy. The area is filled with small companies like ours, mostly in the financial sector.

I come from a family of immigrants. My parents immigrated to Switzerland where they met and married. Then, 59 years ago, I was born. In their newly adopted country, they had the good fortune to learn a skill and adopt a new mindset. It was their wish to pass along their gratitude and work ethic to my brother and me, seasoned with a generous dose of honesty, respect, and duty.

In the financial boom of the 1980s, I set off with my brother to attend an entrepreneurial seminar to investigate starting a business together. With my commercial and administrative abilities and my brother's technical aptitude, we knew we couldn't fail.

In the beginning, our skill sets complemented one another, but then things turned sour. As we spent time together building our company, pressures mounted. Stress, fear, insecurities and bad business advice brought discontent to our small family business. We gave in to our doubts and inexperience.

At times I was racked with guilt because of my bad behavior, especially when I unloaded my stress on my brother. I've since learned that the startup phase of building a company can cause upheaval and drama in your life. It certainly did in mine, which manifested itself physically and mentally. Physically, I gained a lot of weight and was diagnosed with hypertension. Mentally, my continuous mood swings and worries about money created panic attacks and anxiety. Time and time again, I lashed out at my family, leaving them concerned about my wellbeing.

After several years, to avoid the constant disagreements and quarrels, my brother and I decided, by mutual agreement, to hire a third person as a peacemaker, an arbitrator who would listen to both sides to improve the development of our burgeoning company.

This person acted most often as a general manager in charge of the day to day operations, not on making the larger business decisions. His management style created a lot of problems with our management team, and he demotivated many of our employees to the point of leaving the company, in some cases, even after many years of service.

With his termination, we uncovered many of the practices he had instituted during his tenure and how they had detrimentally affected our business. Our search to replace him began. This time around, we wanted to be sure to select a different professional with different characteristics from our previous director. Someone who was better suited to our mentality. Someone with fresher ideas.

At the suggestion of one of our external collaborators, who had already had previous professional experience and excellent results with Monika Ben Thabetova, we decided to schedule a consultation with her.

Before the meeting took place, I decided to cancel. I was skeptical about hiring someone whose business was so trivial, as her specialty was numerology, and I was ignorant of the subject. But our colleague's persistence and insistence convinced us to proceed.

After her presentation, we felt it would be most beneficial if we met with her separately and then wrap up with a joint meeting. Her initial assessment of my birthdate surprised me. Monika's summary of the numbers analysis on my attitudes, my doubts, and my weaknesses hit the mark.

She pointed out things about myself that I thought I actually understood, but I had never accepted. Dark sides of my personality that I didn't even know were there unknowingly made me act impetuously without a real reason.

The next step on my journey with Monika, which in fact became the first in a series of steps, analyzed my thinking. The conclusions pointed out that I had two types of awareness – low and high. The elimination of reaction and the institution of response were her prescription. "Use a period of reflection before you respond in any given situation. Pretend to use a switch that turns off low awareness and turns on high-level awareness. This is an important step toward change," she said. The question I asked most frequently during my phase of reflection was, "How can I act differently?" I must admit, I didn't respond correctly initially. But I was paying attention. I was aware. Another question that came up a lot during this phase was, "What's in the way of correcting my behavior?" Gradually, as the meetings went by, I noticed a slow but steady change in myself.

Everyone, especially the members of my family, remarked on the changes in my behavior. My relationship with my wife and daughters greatly improved. An optimistic serenity began to replace my pessimism. The research into my dogmas, both personal and professional, and the reassessment of my values changed the way I viewed myself.

Now, I live a more peaceful life. Where problems once existed, only learning experiences remain. Mind you, challenges have not completely disappeared, but I view them with positivity, knowing that my values are stronger in every case and will give me the strength and the knowledge to solve them.

If I may give advice to all of those who may find value in it: avoid any initial skepticism about working with Monika. Because the path you undertake with her will be filled with excitement, intensity, and surprises. As you steadily release your old ways, the desire for self-improvement will sprout, forcing you to set aside the negativity that often surrounds you. As much as possible, we must seek better attitudes to improve our lives and relationships with those we share our time.

• • •

Now that you've read the stories of people with various backgrounds who've experienced firsthand the life-changing effects of the table of THE SECRET of NUMBERS, let's get you started doing your own investigation.

As you may have noticed, people continue to thank me or Andrea although I keep saying that I am just communicating what the numbers mean. From this point on, I will be conveying to you a great deal of my knowledge.

Grab your sheet of paper and your pen, and take a deep breath.

Now let's get started!

How to calculate The SECRET of NUMBERS table

Write out your date of birth including day, month, and year in full.

Here is an example birthdate:

May 30, 1976

Always write your numbers in the order of DAY, MONTH, YEAR.

30/05/1976

You may enter your own information or that of a person you're interested in learning more about.

Steps to follow in the exact sequence as described below:

A) Add every number of your birthdate. $3 + 0 + 0 + 5 + 1 + 9 + 7 + 6 = 31$

B) Add up the numbers that makes up the total. 31 becomes $3 + 1 = 4$

C) Write down the total (number 4) of the first result (number 31)

D) Multiply the first number of your birthdate (that's not a zero) by 2 (i.e., $3 \times 2 = 6$)

E) Now subtract that number from the original sum of your birth date (i.e., $31 - 6 = 25$). The total is 25. Write it below the other numbers.

F) Add up the total. 25 becomes $2 + 5 = 7$. Write it below the other numbers.

G) Now you can start filling out YOUR OWN TABLE!

30/05/1976		31
		4
		25
		7

Note: The table will teach you the meaning of the individual numbers that are included in each box.

Note: If the result of the first sum is composed of a single digit, below you will need to repeat the same number.

Example date: 1/1/2001 becomes 1 + 1 + 2 + 1 = 5. Since 5 cannot be added together to give you the second number, just repeat the number by writing it down twice.

The sequence of these numbers will be important.

1/1/2001		5
		5
		3
		3

Caution: In cases where multiplying the first digit of the birthdate results in a number greater than the final sum and when subtracting it would create a negative number, put a zero. To use a number less than zero would make completing the chart impossible. In the example below, when this happens, we replace the last two digits with two 0's.

For instance, January 7, 2000.

7 + 1 + 2 + 0 + 0 + 0 = 10

1+0=1

7 x 2 = 14

10 - 14 = -4

The -4 would become a 0 as will the one below it, making the person a double 0.

7/1/2000		10
		1
		0
		0

Keep in mind that this table reveals very special things about a person's personality. Indigo children are a great example. These children do not interpret reality through their five senses like the rest of us do. Instead, they live on a completely different dimension, mainly utilizing their sixth sense of intuition. And they tend to be proficient in only one thing, such as: drawing, singing, sports, or mathematics. However, their talent may manifest itself in an altogether different area of specialization, such as: a special ability for compassion and understanding of others, being highly emotionally sensitive, or having an exceptional ability for defusing violence.

If you have a child at home with a birthdate containing two zeros, know that they may very well be an indigo child. Please look upon them as more special than royalty. Encourage the expression of their special gift (whatever it may be), because counteracting it could have disastrous effects on their personality and character, not to mention their future. Indigo children have a propensity toward extreme conduct, such as: eating disorders, aggression, hyperactivity or, conversely, total closure, denial, deep insecurity, and muteness. Since their behavior does not conform to what might be considered normal, a parent's tendency might be to pronounce them "sick" or abnormal. Seeking outside help from a doctor because of their "sickness" or "abnormality" could create greater suffering for the child. Accept your child for who and what they are. If you've been chosen to raise such an extraordinary person, it means you must have extraordinary skills yourself.

HOW TO FILL IN THE TABLE

Let's do it together!

Take the time to account for all the digits in your calculations, ending with your total. Following the directions below, we can begin to fill in the chart together.

Be careful to place each of the numbers on the chart as described, because they will ALWAYS go in this same position.

We will fill out our sample table using the above-referenced sample birthdate of May 30, 1976.

$3 + 0 + 0 + 5 + 1 + 9 + 7 + 6 = 31, 4, 25, 7$

- Let's start with box number 1. The top left corner is dedicated to all the 1's you have in your calculations. Simply count the number of 1's from all the digits you've calculated so far, and put them in the box dedicated to the 1's. From our example, there is one 1 in 1976 and another 1 in 31. Place two number 1's in the box dedicated to the 1's.

- Next, count the total number of 2's, and put them in the box dedicated to number 2's. From our example, there is one 2. Write a single 2 in box number 2.

- Count the total number of 3's, and put them in the box dedicated to number 3's. From our example, there are two 3's. Write two 3's in box number 3.

- Count the total number of 4's, and put them in the box dedicated to number 2's. From our example, there is a single 4. Write a single 4 in box number 4.

- Count the total number of 5's, and put them in the box dedicated to number 5's. From our example, there are two 5's. Write two 5's in box number 5.

- Count the total number of 6's, and put them in the box dedicated to number 6's. From our example, there is a single 6. Write a single 6 in box number 6.

- Count the total number of 7's, and put them in the box dedicated to number 7's. From our example, there are two 7's. Write two 7's in box number 7.

- Count the total number of 8's, and put them in the box dedicated to number 8's. From our example, there are no 8's. Write a hyphen (-) in box number 8.*

- Count the total number of 9's, and put them in the box dedicated to number 9's. From our example, there is a single 9. Write a single 9 in box number 9.

*If one of the numbers is missing from your calculations, put a hyphen (-) into the corresponding box. For example, there are no 8's in our calculations. Therefore, you'd put a - in the box dedicated to number 8.

This is the box where you enter all the number 1s	This is the box where you enter all the number 4s	This is the box where you enter all the number 7s	
This is the box where you enter all the number 2s	This is the box where you enter all the number 5s	This is the box where you enter all the number 8s	
This is the box where you enter all the number 3s	This is the box where you enter all the number 6s	This is the box where you enter all the number 9s	

We take the date and the calculations for the birthdate, May 30, 1976.

30/05/1976		31	
		4	
		25	
		7	

11	4	77	
2	55	-	
33	6	9	

Box number 1 has two number 1's.

Box number 2 only has one number 2.

Box number 3 has two number 3's.

Box number 4 has one number 4.

Box number 5 has two number 5's.

Box number 6 has one number 6.

Box number 7 has two number 7's.

Box number 8 has – (a hyphen), because there are no number 8's.

Box number 9 has one number 9. At this point, you may have remarked that numbers are always placed into their dedicated box. It's as easy as that.

And now as you fill in the other blanks, you'll notice a vertical row of blank boxes on the right side of the table:

- Count out the number of digits in each horizontal line.
- Put that total into the empty box on the right for each line.
- Proceed in the same way with the figures present in the subsequent horizontal rows.

We return again to our example.

11	4	77	5
2	55	-	3
33	6	9	4

In the first horizontal line we find:

Two 1's

One 4

Two 7's

Therefore, we count 5 total digits. Put 5 into the empty box on the right.

Do the same thing on the other two horizontal rows.

In the empty boxes on the right, we will write the numbers 3 and 4 (total of the figures contained in the individual horizontal rows).

REMEMBER: only use the total number of digits in each box contained in the horizontal lines, NOT their numerical value.

We calculate the number of digits to fill in the empty boxes below the columns:

It proceeds in exactly the same manner, but this time you count vertically.

Let's count the number of digits in the first column. Count down vertically.

11	4	77	5
2	55	-	3
33	6	9	4
5	4	3	

Two 1's

One 2

Two 3's

For a total of 5

Put 5 in the empty box below the first column.

Fill in the other blank boxes in the same way.

In the empty boxes of the subsequent vertical lines of our example, we will write then the numbers 4 and 3 (total number of digits contained in the individual columns of each).

REMEMBER: Count only the total number of digits contained in the vertical lines and not their numerical value.

Let's begin reading!

I hope you can see that calculating the table is not difficult.

Now stop, take a deep breath, and quiet your mind. You want to look at the table introspectively to allow the flow of information from the numbers to come to you naturally. Try to look into the qualitative value of the numbers. Look past the digits; go below the surface. Looking superficially at the numbers is deceptive and can lead to illusion. This may sound rather ethereal, but just stay with me for a minute. Imagine going into your kitchen. There you find both salt and sugar. On the surface, they look identical, don't they? But we all know they are very different, one from the other. It is the same with the table.

Therefore, approach the table with an open mind. Turn off your brain for a minute, and turn on your intuition, listening to any sensations that may come from your solar plexus level. Pay attention to any images that may come to you.

Throw out any questions like, "Is it possible that the numbers could tell me something?"

I assure you that they will. After more than 25 years of calculating tables and reading people's charts, I know personally that the numbers speak.

Each number attracts a certain energy. What kind of energy?

The significance of each number's energy is explained by the box to which each number belongs. I will get to the explanation shortly.

(It is very important that every number from your calculations is placed in its dedicated box on the table if you want to get an accurate reading.)

Numbers that are repeated have a higher energy.

The presence of more than three identical numbers in the same box indicates an imbalance in that characteristic. An imbalance could manifest itself with symptoms like hyperactivity, stress, tension, and restlessness, etc. If this surplus energy is not channeled properly, it can sometimes become a real problem for the person. Proper ways to channel this excess energy may be through sports, dancing, singing, writing, acting, drawing, or any other physical activity.

If the person does not find a suitable channel, a tendency is to succumb to addictions, which could curtail his power, such as: alcohol, drugs, sex, gambling, or activities that cause adrenaline rushes – anything that dulls the mind and gives a temporary feeling of wellbeing. When the effects wear off, it can cause a person to feel worse than before. They can become aggressive, angry, or act out in destructive ways. To avoid this type of outcome, it's important to pay close attention to the significance of each box in the table and to commit to understanding and channeling your energy appropriately to get positive results in that area.

Another very important thing to understand is that each number has both a positive and a negative side, and that repeated numbers are wonderful gifts if used in a positive way. Unfortunately, it is rare for unaware people to understand the importance of their abilities and qualities. Oftentimes, they'll use their special gifts counterproductively, resulting in frustration, anxiety, and nervousness.

We'll go into more detail in the following pages.

Let's now look at the meaning attached to each box.

Selfishness	Assertiveness	Connection to spirituality and the universe	Determination
Health & Sexuality	Intuition	Suffering	Awareness/ Sensitivity
Order & Flexibility	Decision making ability	Sense of family, roots	Intelligence
Talent & Artistry	Confidence in self & others	Speech, Materialism	

Below are the basic meanings for each box. But reading the numbers does not stop here.

The reading is performed based on:

• the total number of digits in each box.

- missing numbers.

- each number put on a scale.

- using your intuition to understand what each number is communicating.

- how the numbers combine energetically with one another.

Congratulations are in order – you have now learned how to calculate and create your own table of THE SECRET of NUMBERS.

And in the following chapters, you will learn the meaning of each number and how to properly interpret it.

• • •

THE MEANING OF THE BOXES

Box #1 – Selfishness

What is selfishness? We often think that having an ego is a bad thing. In fact, our ego is what makes us "people of the flesh." Ego connects us to reality. It allows us to have a name, a nationality, a skin color, an eye shade, a favorite football or basketball team, a career title, or a college degree. Our identities are derived from it, giving us permission to believe what is written on our birth certificates, driver's licenses, passports, etc. You are probably thinking, "Of course, who else would I be if I didn't have a name, a nationality, or a title?"

That is true but only to a certain point. Because if the ego is used and managed correctly, then we live a peaceful life in balance and in harmony with ourselves. In fact, we use our ego appropriately when using our names to answer the phone, when we sign our name to a document, or when we get a car insurance card. However, if we allow our egos to suffocate us, if we allow it to want to "be right" no matter what instead of doing the right thing in life, then we're going to find ourselves in trouble. When the ego has unlimited control over our thinking, over our life, then we are separated from our true essence, our soul, and our soul's mission. The ego casts a mystical spell over our mind, making us believe we're not responsible for either our mistakes, our choices, or our lives. Our behavior and our decision making process becomes stuck in a conditions-based atmosphere. The strongest influence to our thinking comes from outside ourselves. External forces become our guides to satisfy our ego. **We live from the outside-in instead of from the inside-out**. Nothing more. The ego makes us believe that what we are, what we do, and what we possess should be at the mercy of what others think. In this way, we tie ourselves to that belief. If it so happens that we lose our jobs or we lose our money, then we could become extremely confused, depressed, and angry because the things in our outside world define who we are. The bigger our confusion, our depression, or our anger, the stronger the hold the ego has over us. We will discover the strength of the ego's stronghold over us by looking at the quantity of digits in box number 1. The total number of digits a person has in box number 1 determines how much he thinks of himself. The more numbers, the more he thinks of himself.

If there is no digit in box number 1

These are selfless people who disappear in a crowd. The need to satisfy their own needs also disappears. People like this are easily manipulated and often have a deep sense of guilt. They put the needs of other people before their own, to their own detriment, and at the expense of their own well-being. It is their wish to be kind and give help to anyone who needs it. Asking others for help would be out of the question. But deep down inside, they probably wonder, "If I am doing everything for others, why doesn't anyone else help me?" without realizing their mistake. Selfless people like this often feel alone, isolated, hopeless, and misunderstood.

Observation:

Tables without a digit in box number 1

We find with people born after the year 2000. In fact, these people are not ego driven *per se*. Instead, emotions, feelings, and intuition drive them. They often have a difficult time integrating within a group, spending time contemplating why others aren't more selfless, since it seems so natural for them to think of others first.

One digit in box number 1 (1)

These people are very altruistic, taking great pains to meet the needs of others. Saying NO is often difficult for them. For example, helicopter mothers (those who hover over their child) usually don't realize that they're smothering their child and stifling their decision making ability later in life. These people may be readily crushed or manipulated when others use guilt on them to get their way. They are people who feel a deep need to care for others – either another person or an animal.

Two digits in box number 1 (11)

These people have a great ability to protect themselves from others. Although they willingly put the well-being of others before their own, they will take care of themselves as well. Saying no to others when it doesn't work for them or if something doesn't feel "right" or "good" is not uncommon.

Three digits in box number 1 (111)

It is here where the ego begins to rise, and we can say that the important thing is that these are people who think about themselves first. Their own well-being or their own suffering is their primary concern instead of what others may face. People with one or two digits in box number 1 feel the misfortune, adversity, discomfort, and hardship of others, and want to help them first. But for people who begin to have three digits in box number 1, the situation is reversed. They can sense the pain of others, but this is mainly linked to their own egos.

Four number 1's in the box (1111)

From here, we begin to meet people who reflect well upon whether something will benefit them before saying yes to anything. They are good, kind, and helpful people – the only difference being that behind any decision, they look out for themselves without even realizing this characteristic. In fact, they believe they are doing things for others, and that's it. If you are invited to drink coffee with a person who has 4 digits in box number 1, know they are not doing this to benefit you but, above all, to benefit themselves. Perhaps they're doing it because they like your company or they want to have a good time. These people truly believe in the concept of win-win. However, they can unknowingly manipulate others to fulfill their needs if they're not aware of their true natures.

Five or more number 1's the box (11111)

Unfortunately, these people smile at you, wave at you, hug you, do something for you, but only for their own benefit. They don't have the slightest interest in knowing how you are, what you do, how you feel, or who you are. Without scruples, they don't even understand what it means to have feelings of guilt. These people suffer a lot, because they do recognize their own selfishness, self-centeredness, and coldness, but they're unaware of what to do about it. There are times that they'll stop and reflect on their behavior – they want to improve how they treat others, but again, they succumb to their ego's needs. This happens because they don't readily know how to do things differently. So they return to thinking only of themselves like a snake biting its tail in a vicious circle of the ego. People with 5 or more digits in box number 1 only listen their minds, forgetting their hearts. And if the time comes that it appears their heart takes charge, it won't last long.

They once again become absorbed by their egos. They may manipulate others to get what they want without even realizing that they're doing it. It is often that they give others ultimatums, backing them into corners, making them think it's benefitting them when in fact their wellbeing isn't even in the equation. In any situation, the fact is they are not the manipulated but rather the manipulators.

So far you've learned to understand why it is important to know how many numbers are in box number 1 about selfishness in the table of THE SECRET of NUMBERS. However, this box must be read in conjunction with other numbers in other boxes. Selfishness can be experienced in different ways depending on its strength and the power of the other numbers.

If by chance you have many number 1's in your chart, take a moment to stop and ponder this. It is imperative that you begin directing that strong energy in a positive way. Remember the great law of the universe: for every action there is an equal and opposite reaction... even if the action is only a thought.

• • •

Box #2 – Health and Sexuality

What is health and sexuality? Despite being one of the most important, this box is somewhat taboo. In society, speaking of our intimacy, our sexuality, of what we like to do or how and how many times is a no-no. If we talk openly about it, we are taught to feel ashamed or embarrassed. We might even turn red, even though sexuality is the lever that moves the world. Thanks to having sex, making love, and being in intimate physical contact with another, we reproduce, maintaining human life on planet Earth. And we're not supposed to talk about it! Why is that? Doesn't it seem absurd? Yes, it does!

Let's see how the table of THE SECRET of NUMBERS interprets the level of health and sexuality of each individual.

If there is no digit in box number 2

People with no digits in box number 2 must pay particular attention to their own health, being more attentive to the food they eat and the exercise they perform. They should never ignore physical problems that present themselves or if they're confronted by some sort of physical ailment. These people shouldn't drink alcohol, smoke cigarettes, or do drugs, committing instead to a healthy and balanced lifestyle. Their bodies can be more susceptible to disease and ailments. Drinking alcohol or smoking cigarettes causes more damage in these people than it does in others, because it takes much longer for their bodies to process these toxins. Therefore, it is strongly recommended they avoid all harmful substances, even in moderation.

Sex to these people is not a fundamental part of life, and oftentimes, they do not like physical contact. They may seem cold and detached. They do not particularly like hugs, kisses, or any sort of tenderness.

Observation:

Box number 2 is closely linked to box number 8, more of which will be explained later about why a person who has no number 2's but has number 8's should pay closer attention to his health – particularly in regards to his sexuality. He prefers the mental sexual activity full of emotions and passion more than he does the physical act.

One digit in box number 2 (2)

These people should also protect their health, maintaining a healthy and balanced lifestyle. Obviously, they'll believe they should be able to do everything life has to offer, and they're completely right. But there are certain people who are more vulnerable than others, who are stronger. Even tender caresses or too many touches are not fundamental for these people to live a life in which they feel loved. Sex is not an important issue for them in everyday life. In fact, people with one digit in box number 2 can live in abstinence for long periods.

Two digits in box number 2 (22)

Here we begin to see people who are very healthy. Nothing throws them off course. For this type of person, sickness or disease is rarely linked to the physical; it is often linked to the psyche. Their illnesses are usually psycho-somatic in nature.

When people have two digits in box number 2, we begin to see sex as an important component in everyday life. They need physical contact, caresses, hugs, kisses, and to feel wanted. They want another person's physical presence, be it a friend or a partner.

Three digits in box number 2 (222)

When these people are close to someone else, they feel compelled to touch, to feel, and to have real physical contact with that person. It is often very apparent from a young age. Children who have more number 2's need to be held by their parents much more than others do. This is a very important thing to understand particularly during adolescence. As a child enters his teenage years, he begins to explore his sexuality, noticing the changes taking place in his body. If at home the topic of sex is a taboo, as is the case in most households, this teenager will begin to seek affection outside of the home. But if parents are aware of their child's higher sex drive, they can transmit their love his way, having discussions with him about what a beautiful thing sex is. If this becomes the case, he will not have the need to go outside the house to look for confirmation from others, routinely expressed sexually. People with three digits in box number 3 love cuddles, hugs, kisses, and holding hands. They need to make love more often. Therefore, it is very important and that their partner knows this, because if they do not meet this need, this instinct, they could begin to close in on themselves, repressing their feelings, and convincing themselves that they are actually no good. In time, their unmet needs can manifest themselves as illness or by acting out aggressively.

Note: When you get three number 2's in this box, sexual energy exceeds that of health. In relationships that are not physical or sexual in nature, but platonic, i.e., friendship, work, etc., they could be very affectionate. If one is not aware of this quality, these relationships risk becoming misunderstood by one or both parties or by people outside the relationship.

Four numbers in box 2 (2222)

For these people physical contact and sexual intercourse are fundamental and important. When choosing a life partner, People with four numbers in box number 2 should take into consideration this characteristic. They need to have a partner with the same level of sexual drive as they do to fulfill their physical needs as well as their fantasies. Otherwise, these people risk breaking down and are likely to get sick. Their sensibility is truly remarkable.

Five or more numbers in the box 2 (22222)

The sexual charge of these people is really high. They are extremely sensitive to the sexual needs of others without being asked. For them, physical contact is essential; they would die without it. They want to caress and be caressed, to embrace and be embraced, to kiss and be kissed. They are very affectionate and warm. Understanding this characteristic without judging them for it is essential.

Comments: Imagine that there was a person born with a high sex drive and another with very little sex drive at all. I do not want you to think that there is something right or wrong in either case. We are not all equal and never will be; that's part of the beauty of life. People with low sex drives have other qualities that those with high drives don't. No one is the same. It doesn't mean that people with a lot of digits in the number 2 box are necessarily promiscuous. These people remain loyal to their partners as long as their needs are being met. Otherwise, they risk feeling suffocated in the relationship.

Think about two people who meet and fall in love. One has no digits in box number 2 while the other has four. They stay together, because they're in love. But for months or years, they've felt like something wasn't right between them, like something was missing. The person with many number 2's because of his high sex drive, needs to make love often, while the other person, despite the love, doesn't have the same needs. Problems like conflicts, betrayals, misunderstandings, accusations, and divorce come to pass. Isn't it obvious how important this knowledge in a couple's intimate relationship could be?

Another thing to understand about box number 2 is that it is an especially important component in the life of every individual, because in reality, sex is energy. If this energy flows freely, all other aspects of life will run smoothly. But if this type of energy is blocked, all other things in life have the potential to come crashing down.

Remarks: I would like to write a note on children and sex. Children born from 2000 and beyond are completely different children simply due to the fact that their birth year no longer begins with the number 1. This means they will always have at least one number 2 in their charts. For this reason, these people really need affection so much more than

those of us born before 1999. They need to have physical touch and to stay in constant contact. Those of us who are parents born in the 1900s aren't like them. Often we do not understand them. We judge their behavior, continuously comparing it to our own. If we're not aware of this slight variation in the numbers, it will simply drive them away from us as parents, sending them straight into the arms of someone else who might abuse them. If you're the parent of a child born after 2000, I invite you to reflect upon this, and understand the great need of your children for physical contact with you. However, if you have raised your child thus far with a certain detachment, you cannot expect them to accept your sudden attempts now out of the blue to start hugging, cuddling, or kissing them. Just try to observe and understand them in this new way. If you do, you will have already made great strides toward reducing the problem of child sexuality.

So far, you've learned to understand why it is important to know why box number 2 – health and sexuality – is so important in the table of THE SECRET of NUMBERS.

However, this box must be read in conjunction with the energies of other numbers. When you take into consideration how their energies commingle, it changes the role of health and sexuality. Depending on the number of digits in that box, you will see how it can manifest itself in different ways. More on this later.

• • •

Box #3 – Order and Flexibility

What does order & flexibility mean?

Let's take a look at the meaning of these words.

Order: To be endowed with the special gift of being able to see things that are out of place. To have a great disposition to notice details. Grasping or understanding what's right or wrong in any situation at a glance. Having the ability to quickly assess the reality around us.

Flexibility: When we encounter a situation in life, whether positive or negative, flexibility is the one gift that pushes us to accept it for what it is. This does not mean that we accept all circumstances blindly, especially if they lead to pain or suffering, but we commit to constructively understanding everything that shows up. In knowing how to be flexible lies an immense force. Thanks to our ability to be flexible, we learn to accept the sun and the rain, heat and cold, because everything has some positive aspect to offer. If, instead of rigidity, we chose flexibility in our everyday lives, we would encounter much less conflict, pain, and suffering. When we experience pain, we want to get rid of it as quickly as possible. Flexibility allows us to address life's circumstances, projecting our thoughts beyond our person. In this way, we become more and more capable of realizing that every event, whether positive or negative, becomes an opportunity to enrich our souls. Stress arises, restricting people's emotions and events, when the mind doesn't accept what life puts in front of us. When we analyze things that happen to us, we begin to reap potential lessons that, in the long term, can make us stronger, wiser, and more sensitive. We drop our expectations and judge every event without the ramblings of critical self-talk. We accept things for what they are and what they really look like. When we welcome flexibility, we learn to rejoice even in difficult or sad situations, such as a foreclosure, a bankruptcy, or the end of an intimate relationship. In fact, the term flexibility can also be understood as a profound awareness of the fact that there are two sides to everything in life – front and back, black and white, on and off. But in order to live in peace, it's better to focus on the positive sides of an issue. Such as, when a relationship ends, instead of focusing on the pain and despair, choose to be lucid and appreciative of the fact that it opens the possibility for a new romance. Flexibility means being adaptable and elastic, so we are able to be malleable in every situation much like the way water takes the shape of the vessel that contains it.

If there is no digit in box number 3

These people live by the motto, "Live and let live." They don't claim to have anything on anyone, professing to be open, tolerant, and flexible instead. Sometimes it could get messy, not only in their home life, but in all areas of their lives. They do not criticize anyone, and they especially don't want to be criticized for the simple fact that they want peace and harmony around them, without someone telling them what, when, and how they should do something. We can easily hear them say, "But that's okay." They are easily manipulated. But when they realize this, they push the manipulator away abruptly. Seeing things displaced or out of place is not their strong suit, and we certainly can't expect them to maintain order. It's much better for them to live with disorder and chaos.

One digit in box number 3 (3)

These people will go with the flow rather easily, until they see something out of place. That's when they'll stop and reevaluate a given situation. Their flexibility allows them to sit calmly and with absolute peace in the middle of the opinions of others, and listen, discussing openly differing viewpoints. They are not rooted in or convinced by what they believe to be the truth.

Two digits in box number 3 (33)

The people with two digits in box number 3 start to expect order and discipline around them, and although they claim they need them both, they're not necessarily always able to maintain it. In discussions, they often want to have the last word, and sometimes they find it hard to compromise. However, they're still willing to take a step back, look at a situation in a detached manner, and to keep the peace even if it causes their own inner struggle. They have the analytical talent of recognizing when things are out of place and the ability to put them back into order.

Three digits in box number 3 (333)

Here we begin to see a real lack of flexibility, encountering rigid people. At first glance, they appear very intelligent and capable of civilly exchanging in dialogue. But in the end, they must have the last word. They can ruin any discussion, remaining fully engaged to prove that they are right at any cost. In the heat of the moment, their sole objective is to fog the mind of their "opponent" to convince them of the truth. But, alas, the peace and beauty around them gets lost, and people's feelings can get hurt. This way of dealing with life often leads people to having a tremendous amount of inner tension incapable of relaxation. They are perfectionists and expect perfection in others as well.

Four digits in box number 3 (3333)

These people are obsessive, demanding absolute order, and if they don't get it, they become angry, irritable, and upset. They do not recognize how off putting this behavior comes across to others. They have high expectations when it comes to others. Everyone and everything gets judged, and, above all, they subconsciously judge themselves harshly. Being right is a way of life. Without exception, they want to have the last word, being unwilling to accept the opposing views of other people. They are extremely rigid know-it-alls. They want to give everyone advice about everything always, because they think they know the best way of doing all things. Under no circumstances are they capable of accepting criticism from others. Their stance when confronted with criticism is to immediately become defensive. They do truly have the great gift of understanding and seeing situations from a different perspective, but unfortunately, they often fall into the trap of destructive criticism, alienating others. When this happens, they don't understand the real reason why people become alienated since all they were trying to do is to help and give advice.

Box number 3 is directly tied to box number 4 in the table of THE SECRET of NUMBERS. People blessed with digits in box number 4 have the unique ability to say anything they think without creating any problem or conflicts.

In the section on box number 3, you learned to understand why it is important to know how many digits are in box number 3 for order and flexibility in your chart of THE SECRET of NUMBERS. However, this box must be read in conjunction with other numbers to determine your order and flexibility in life.

And if you're a person with three or more digits in box number 3, I'd like you to stop and ponder this for a moment. Because of the unfortunate fact that the power of 3 plays out more often in destructive capacity rather than a constructive one. Remember that the Pareto principle (also known as the 80/20 rule) states that, for many events, roughly 80% of the effects come from 20% of the causes and not vice versa. If you apply this idea to the role number 3's play, then you will understand that your life will never be the same.

• • •

Box #4 – Assertiveness

What is assertiveness?

Assertiveness is the ability for a person to externalize his emotions, views, and ideas freely without worrying about the opinions of others or their reactions. When a person has an idea or a thought, assertive people feel the need to say directly how they feel or what they think, sometimes speaking too directly and hurting the feelings of people around them without even realizing it.

If there is no digit in box number 4

People who have no digits in box number 4 never say what they think or how they feel. We can never understand what goes on in the back of their minds. Often, with a smile they say that everything is fine, when in actuality, this isn't the case. They have a tendency to bottle up unexpressed feelings and unspoken words for many years, which they may have turned into "injustices" against them in their minds. They stifle their emotions, believing that others know what they want or what they don't want without ever saying a word. Then when they get or don't get what they wanted or didn't want, or they get something they didn't expect, they can shut down. Or, conversely, they could explode. These people are prone to false dependencies such as alcohol, drugs, compulsive shopping, workaholism, money, power, or sex. They don't realize, however, these compulsions will never fill the void they feel inside.

Observation:

Our addictions are how we try to fill the emptiness we feel within us. In reality, this vacuum can only be filled by things we really need. The most important ones being that which is connected to our spirituality, our close contact with nature, loving relationships with other human beings, the sense of accomplishment in our work, and the feeling that we are contributing, either within our family, our community, our city or on a global scale. But if we are to meet these needs, the first step is being able to recognize them and become aware that these are important to living a fulfilled life.

One digit in box number 4 (4)

These are people who assert their own points of view and express their opinions without overpowering others. They are clear, direct, and capable of being themselves in any situation and saying directly what they think and want. These people are natural leaders, oftentimes, without being aware that others are following them. They always say what they think, and if they see an injustice, they feel the need to speak up or to intervene.

Two digits in box number 4 (44)

Here we begin to see people expressing stronger personal points of view. They will listen to the opinions of others, but, in the end, they will always do what they want. These people are more rigid. When they have an opinion about something, it is almost impossible to change their mind. They are willing to "fight" to prove that they are right, quickly defending their ideology to the point of forgetting they are not "their" ideology. As self-righteous people who seek to apply what they believe everywhere, they don't realize that not everyone is interested in being helped. They are great leaders but, unfortunately, too hard and expect to be respected by force instead of from earning it. They should keep in mind that no one follows a true leader because of what he says but for what he does.

Three digits in box number 4 (444)

People with three digits in box number 4 are, you know, a little different. They live in their world. Often they do not speak to others, and they don't feel the need to share their opinions, emotions, or feelings with others because they're essentially not interested in what they think. In the company of others, they may feel uncomfortable, because they don't understand or feel understood. Children with this type of behavior may feel the most uncomfortable, because we demand that they communicate in the same way everyone else does, but they are not capable of doing it. This is why, when they are forced against their will to speak or participate in a group, they become aggressive. Once someone becomes aggressive, they get a lot of attention, and from then on, they are viewed differently. Unfortunately, as children, they end up being treated with psychotropic drugs in the hopes that they become "normal." As adults, they may continue to seek psychological therapy because their behavior bears no resemblance to that of other people. Conversely, when they do speak, they tend to talk a lot with a strongly dictatorial manner of speaking, which can turn other people off. Another tendency is their struggle with authority and the rule of law, because in their opinion, they make their own rules. No one tells them what to do. In fact, these people should not be disturbed or provoked. They just need to be left in peace and helped, so that over time, they can discover what they like to do and what they want to do in "their world." If you encounter these types of people, let them be; observe them from a distance without suffocating them. With the right approach, they can learn to understand their stiffness, and their rigidity can become an invincible tool to get what they want when it is used in a positive way. They can become great leaders and entrepreneurs, contributing to helping change the circumstances around them in a very powerful way.

Four or more digits in box number 4 (4444)

These people are very rare cases. There have been only a very few times in which I have met people with four or more digits in box number 4 for an appointment. They were very difficult to approach because they cannot communicate. To say they are different from everybody else would be a true statement. But to label them as abnormal, the way it is negatively used in today's society, would do them a disservice. However, they are not normal, meaning not regular or usual like the rest of us. They are just not the same. And for this, they are perceived differently and are recognized as having symptoms of mental illness. To this end, they are almost always under the care of a psychiatrist who prescribes them medication.

Note: If you are a psychiatrist or a psychotherapist, the very fact that you are reading this book tells me that you are willing to recognize that what you have been taught by scientific books is not all there is in your profession. You have probably realized that there is something else at work in life that has a great deal of power. You recognize that there are other tools available that go further into the depths of a human being to better understand his psyche. You feel that your one and only mission is to help your patients in the best possible way. Congratulations for having decided to get closer to the ancient science of numbers.

In the section about box number 4, you learned to understand why it is important to know how many 4's there are in box number 4 on assertiveness from the table of THE SECRET of NUMBERS. However, this box must be read in conjunction with the other numbers and depending on the level of assertiveness, its meaning can be transformed.

Box #5 – Intuition

Intuition

Since our births, each of us has had the ability to use our intuition. But, unfortunately, in our society we stifle this wonderful gift. Many of us have trained our intellects to question our own insights. When we have an intuitive feeling, 95% of the time, our minds reject it saying, "I do not think it will work," or "What a crazy idea that came to mind." And so, your intuition gets turned off and pushed aside. It is very important to train your intellect to observe, listen, and express its inner voice – your intuitive voice. Luckily, there are people who have developed their intuitive gift in a profound way, and despite living in a society based on the "cult of rationality," they can tune into and hear what their intuition has to say. If you develop your own intuitive gift, it could help you in all areas of your life. It could help you to process information, make decisions, to take care of yourself, and interact positively with others. Knowing how to listen to our intuition makes even our most relaxing days even more pleasant. In paying attention more often, our inner voice will begin to speak louder, clearer, and more often, thus becoming an effective and trusted guide in our lives. If you learn to listen to it, you won't need to ask for advice from anyone else ever again.

If there is no digit in box number 5

These people have a greater tendency to listen to their rational mind, behaving a little bit like the computer. They process inputs that come from outside and, based on the information received, draw logical conclusions. Actually, they have big limitations within themselves, because you only rely on direct experiences they've had in their lives and the knowledge gained through their five senses.

A single digit in box number 5 (5)

Here we begin to see people who on occasion have flashes of intuition, but still tend to ignore them, keeping their inner voice locked away in a corner somewhere deep inside themselves. And sometimes, when they use it, without realizing that it is their inner voice guiding them, they are amazed at how beneficial it has been to them or their situation. "Perhaps," they say, "it was luck or destiny…" Their inclination is to always give credit to something external instead of understanding that it was their inner voice, their own personal intuitive gift, that enlightened them about which path to take or which choice to make.

Two digits in box number 5 (55)

These people have already tapped into their much sharper intuition. They comprehend that they have access to "certain information," because at times they anticipate a situation by trusting a feeling they have inside themselves as if they already knew the outcome. Unwittingly, they manage to "guess" the future, and if they recognize this fact and can trust it, the possibility exists for them to have the ability to anticipate what will happen for others too. At times, this leads them to garner an inner tranquility. Despite being in the middle of a dark period in their lives, they can step outside the situation and, from a distance, see ahead and know everything will work out in the long run. Through sensitivity and observation, they can sense the invisible world of emotions, feelings, and moods to understand challenges and hardships that others may have faced in the past.

Three digits in box number 5 (555)

Here we begin to see people who can understand and feel what others feel on an even deeper level. They do not need promptings or validation to tune in; it just comes to them in a natural way. If people with three digits in box number 5 recognize the great intuitive gift within themselves and allow themselves to be guided by it, they won't be inclined to make bad or wrong choices, both in their private and professional worlds. For example, at times, these people don't even need to read an agreement or a proposal to know if it's a "good deal." Instead, they trust their instincts.

Four, five, and more digits in box number 5 (5555)

These people are very special, with the true ability to understand things before they happen. Knowing their incredible gift of intuition, they should rely on it blindly. Their choices and instincts will be so accurate that it will appear that they always follow the right path. Their intuitive mind has access to the infinite intelligence in the universe, connecting to an unlimited amount of information without even having experienced it firsthand in their own lives. As very sensitive, intuitive people, others won't be able to hide anything from them. They don't need to hear someone else's story firsthand to know it; they sense it, feel it. By working with subtle energies, they don't even need to take courses or enlist the guidance of a mentor, because they have this thing already within themselves. There are times when they will seek outside training, but this is mostly because they were raised in a family who were deeply rooted in the "cult of rationality", and they are just trying to confirm the fact that invisible intuition exists.

In this section, you've learned to understand the importance of knowing how many five numbers are in box number 5 (intuition) of the table of THE SECRET of NUMBERS.

However, this box, like every other box, must be read in conjunction with the energy of the other numbers and, depending on the degree of intuition of an individual, the results may manifest themselves differently than described above.

If you're someone without a number 5 in the table, don't be concerned. You surely have other, more developed qualities. The only thing that I invite you to do is, if you're in the inner circle of your family, or friends, of people who have number 5's in their table, when making important decision, seek their counsel. If you're not sure what direction to go in any given situation, call them, assess the situation, and rely on their intuition. They offer great insights into your particular situation and give you great options that you would probably not have thought of on your own.

• • •

Box #6 – Power to decide

Power to decide

In my opinion, there are two ways to make a decision.

The impulsive decision, unfortunately, is a decision made quickly, without proper analysis, reached by merely listening to one's mind, one's ego. It's as if the decision were made impetuously and superficially by saying, "Cool, let's do it." Decisions like this don't have a deep foundation and can be those which we later regret. Rarely do we feel secure in these decisions, leading our second guessing ourselves. Our rational minds think we should proceed logically and continuously, from point A to point B to point C. We hope our paths will proceed smoothly, effortlessly, and progressively in a linear fashion. But if this happens, in reality, we never learn anything; we need to evolve.

The intuitive decision is a decision linked to the intuition that we discussed in the previous section. It's a decision in which we enlist the assistance of our inner voice. It's the inner voice that we follow even if it makes us walk down a new and uncomfortable pathway where we didn't expect to go. However, we rely on our inner guidance system. We trust it is conspiring to give us our highest good. It is committed to continually leading us down a path of growth toward our maximum evolution. Sometimes, it tosses us painful challenges that we had probably hoped to avoid, but we know and sense that it is for our own good.

If there is no digit in box number 6

These are the undecided people; those who can never make a decision for themselves. They're afraid to commit to a decision for fear of making mistakes or being wrong. For this, when they are forced to make a decision, it tends to be impulsive. Or they might get a recommendation from someone else, even if it's only indirectly, because they rely on influences and circumstances outside themselves. It's unfortunate how often they change their minds based on what they hear around themselves. For example, if someone with no digits in box number 6 needed to buy a new car, they'd listen to the many opinions of others before committing to a purchase. In the end, as they drive their new car home for the first time, they'll already be looking around, second guessing and finding faults with their decision. Others easily influence or manipulate these people.

A single digit in box number 6 (6)

These people begin to discern whether or not they should listen to the opinions of others. They may sense their own feelings and reflections, but, ultimately, they'll still have a tendency to follow the suggestions of others, unable to trust their own choices. Single digit number 6's are still easily influenced by others.

Two digits in box number 6 (66)

Here we find people who, if they have to make a decision, don't take much time to do it .They look at a situation, evaluate it, and decide. And they don't usually understand why it may have taken others so long to make a decision. They made be heard uttering words like, "The situation seems so clear, does it not?"

Three digits in box number 6 (666)

The mental process of these people is very fast. When faced with a choice, they do not hesitate in reaching their decision immediately. For example, if they see a person who is drowning, even though they may be dressed with a small child in the stroller and unable to swim, they'll throw themselves into the water for the rescue. This is good decision-making speed! People like this are not influenced by others in the slightest; they're sure of their decision making abilities. They are people who make decisions very quickly, immediately assessing a situation and quickly knowing whether to do it or not. However, it's important these people are careful to fully assess any given situation, thinking it all the way through to the end, to reach a proper answer to avoid a painful or difficult outcome.

Four or more digits in box number 6 (6666)

The speed in which these people make decisions can make the heads of other people spin. They decide at lightning speed! For example, if they entered a store to buy something, they'd go directly to the object, grab it, head straight to the cashier and pay. No muss, no fuss. Sometimes, when men are forced to spend hours at a mall shopping with a woman, they might say, "Why do all women love taking so much time to shop?" Now it's clear that this generalization is false, because it doesn't matter whether it's a male or female that determines how a person shops, but rather it depends on how many number 6's one has in their table. These people are used to deciding by using their minds.

In section 6, you've learned to understand why it is important to know how many number 6's you have in box number 6 on the table of THE SECRET of NUMBERS. However, this box is to be read in conjunction with the energy of other numbers.

• • •

Box #7 – Connection to spirituality and the universe

Connection to spirituality and the universe

Box number 7 represents a person's level of access to spirituality and the universe, but the title is not a very accurate definition. It means to admit that there is "something" bigger than yourself, acknowledging the existence of a force greater than you which guides you along your path. You can call it universal intelligence, the Light, God, or any other name that you choose. After all, the name we assign it doesn't really matter. What really matters is whether a person connecting to this ENERGY acknowledges that he doesn't act on his own but has the assistance of an invisible energy that's omnipotent, ever-present, and everywhere. This person surrenders to this energy, becoming a channel through which it flows. It is very important that the message coming through the channel is pure, positive, and to help others around them to feel better, to awaken, and to take them on an inner journey toward awareness. Essentially, you must understand and realize that everything we see and perceive through our five senses has another very important level in another dimension that somehow acts behind the scenes in an invisible world. It would be like looking at a tree and seeing its sturdy trunk, long branches, and canopy of green leaves. But below ground, invisible to the naked eye, the roots reach into the earth far, deep, and wide. You cannot see them, but you know they are there underneath in the dirt. However, if the roots were not there, the tree could not exist. And so it is with everything that surrounds us, everything on the invisible side – where thoughts come from.

THOUGHTS BECOME THINGS. I know it's not the first time you have read this sentence; I am only including it so you never forget it. Therefore, the connection to spirituality is the ability to access higher levels of consciousness. The number seven also represents the universe protecting us.

Observation:

The important thing to know is that people who have the number 7 in the box can be highly spiritual or, on the contrary, be highly realistic and very close to materialism. When people are "realistic," they seek evidence to prove that the invisible does not exist, even though inside they know it does. Generally, they won't acknowledge, or will refuse to admit its existence, until the day when the universe brings a real-life situation that forces them to start believing there is something between the earth and sky. Until that moment, these people repress or avoid the calling toward spirituality and to the invisible world. To suppress the existence of this higher power consumes a lot of energy. Quashing this voice of life will make you pay the price later on in the form of health problems, premature aging, and failure in all spheres of your personal life.

The real reason a person must listen to this inner spiritual voice is to understand that as human beings, we are called to pay attention to our spirit talking to or through us instead of living our whole life rejecting it or pushing it away.

If there is no digit in box number 7

People like this are those who are not connected directly to the universe but have learned everything from books or from the outside, even if they feel their own spirituality. Deep down, they believe that, in life, they must roll up their sleeves and make their own way all by themselves without the universe's help. Their world is a rational one, and their motto in life is, "I believe in what I see." Although they spend much of their time searching for a true connection, it unfortunately never comes.

A single digit in box number 7 (7)

These people are compelled to seek out a connection with their own spirituality but find themselves in a constant struggle whether to believe in the invisible or not. Every now and again, they recognize this as being the hardest fight of their life, since they want to admit to the existence of a force greater than themselves. Alternatively, they may be people who understand that they are related to the spiritual world and somehow feel that they would like to feel more connected to it, but so often they fail.

Two digits in box number 7 (77)

These people start connecting with the subtle energies all around them and develop a certain sensitivity that helps them in their everyday life. They are the people protected by the universe. And if they integrate this "thing" that lives and breathes deeply within them, they begin their life in a constant state of peace. Even if they were having difficult times in their life, they'd always turn their situation around for the better by trusting in the role the universe plays, for it will never disappoint them. When this characteristic is acknowledged and embraced, these people wake up, and become guides for the awakening of others.

Three digits in box number 7 (777)

People with three number 7's are highly energetic universal beings. They have the comportment to be spiritual guides who help others with gesture as simple as a word, a look, or a caress. Unfortunately, they often don't even realize they have the gift of being deeply connected to the universe in the material world, nor do they use it. It may always appear that they are kissed by good fortune, they are lucky, or are in the right place at the right time. At times, they may take advantage of this good fortune, feeling entitled or somehow superior to others, believing that all they've managed to do in life, all they've received, has purely been of their own doing. Of course, this belief is incorrect. The credit belongs to the energy bestowed upon them by the universe, and they are merely channels of it.

Four or more digits in box number 7 (7777)

Here we can see real enlightenment in people possessing four or more number 4's. Unfortunately, it is often wasted on people because they're totally unaware of the gift they possess. They shut down the voice calling them to do things bigger than the trivial business that terrestrial life offers them. But if they recognize their gift, and become strongly connected to their purpose, along with the energy of the universe, they will live their full potential of becoming a pure channel between the physical and the invisible. With this acceptance, they can live out their only purpose while being on the planet.

In Section 7, you've learned to understand the importance of knowing the significance of the number of 7's located in box number 7, and its connection to spirituality and the universe, in the table of THE SECRET of NUMBERS.

However, like all other boxes, it must be read together with the other numbers and based on one's level of access to the spiritual realm.

Observation: Once people with the number 7 in their tables have had their personal spiritual awakening, they then feel compelled to help others experience an equivalent awakening of their own. The term "spiritual awakening" is often misunderstood. It is thought that people who have "paranormal" abilities, or those who are able to channel or can heal others, are spiritually awake. That, of course, is not always the case.

Whoever has not had his own "awakening" is guided and totally identifies with his mind and his ego. Most likely, an inner voice speaks to him incessantly, and he is without the capacity of quieting it. This creates a deep malaise of dark thoughts. These thoughts do nothing but condition him and prevent him from seeing and perceiving the truth that surrounds him; they keep him from knowing what really and truly is. The vision he has of himself is in fact distorted, one that is reduced to mental labels, judgments, opinions, and self-limiting beliefs.

Inside each of us lives two small voices who chatter on and on constantly. You may ask, "What are they?" The answer is very simple – the head and the heart.

Spiritual awakening is usually a gradual process that doesn't happen overnight. Oftentimes, it's brought on by a profound and intense suffering – perhaps the loss of a loved one, an illness, an accident, or a traumatic divorce.

How do I recognize it? The first indication of a spiritual awakening is when you become aware of your thoughts. Realize that you start to notice what you are noticing, a sort of witness to what you are thinking. We do not identify with our minds nor do we identify with the first thought that comes to mind. Instead, it is when we are able to watch ourselves from a distance as if we're outside of ourselves, as if our life were a movie. When this happens, you will discover an immense depth within yourself like one you've never known before. This gives you a wonderful feeling of freedom.

• • •

Box #8 – Suffering

Suffering

Life is not a quiet road that leads to guaranteed happiness, nor is it a straight road without obstacles. In fact, it is almost always the opposite. We must be aware that in life, there are always situations that will make us experience emotions from which we should learn. Suffering is one of these "masters." Probably the best teachers of all and also the most ruthless. It is said that those who have never suffered have never lived.

We all have to learn from our mistakes and failures. Only by learning from these mistakes will we find out the hard way that life is actually a continuous experience of learning that takes us a step closer to fulfilling our journey of personal evolution. Suffering is a very hard thing to deal with, as we all know. But keep in mind that we must never build a wall around ourselves, isolating us from the very pain that will brings us growth. Self-esteem, confidence, and inner strength are the engines that will help us to overcome any suffering.

If there is no digit in box number 8

When these people decide something, they do it without any ifs, ands, or buts. Do you want to know why? Why don't they see any problems or obstacles with what they do? Because if they decided, at this very moment, to leave for any destination, to pack a suitcase this instant, and head out the door, they don't see a problem with it. They are spontaneous beyond measure. There isn't a word to describe them; it doesn't exist. They are fast and claim their speed. For them, the time to do a particular thing is now. They do not see problems anywhere and, if by chance one arises, they resolve it without being attached to the past. They are proactive people. And they are able to live here and now in the present moment.

A single digit in box number 8 (8)

Before taking action, these people have a tendency to wait for the right time. They may start to find small problems that don't exist, because they think it's impossible to do things without finding at least one obstacle. They think it is difficult for things to run smoothly without the slightest stumble. At times, they may be tempted to focus on the negative. Their tendency to live in the fear of the future may show up.

Two digits in box number 8 (88)

These are people who are beginning to be closely linked to their mind, their ego and, consequently, they have a tendency to create imaginary problems, problems that are not actually there. They hold onto the past and struggle to detach from it. Often they wallow in the past or worry about their future instead of focusing on the truth – life is now, at this very moment, in the present.

Anxiety and mood swings often plague them because all their fears and worries lead them to a sort of suffering that they've completely created in their own minds. They think that in order to be happy, you must suffer in life. Sometimes, they can be pessimistic. For this, you have to understand and encourage them.

Three digits in box number 8 (888)

These people may suffer from more depression due to their active imaginations. They are often sick and unable to identify the real reason why. It so happens that they attach to an episode from the past to justify to themselves their poor state of mind. They often try to conceal all this with a fake smile. But, eventually, it all breaks down, and they get sick. Anything can cause them to suffer. Just by looking at the world around them, they think life is unfair. They need someone on their side who understands their state of mind. There may be a tendency in them to hurt other people because they believe "the world has to suffer."

Four or more digits in box number 8 (8888)

Here we may encounter serious problems with depression. These individuals can end up being prescribed psychiatric drugs or turning to other alternatives, such as; sleeping pills, drugs, or alcohol to drown their sorrows.

In section number 8, you've learned why it is important to know how many number 8's are in the suffering box of the table of THE SECRET of NUMBERS.

However, this box is to be read in conjunction with the other numbers in the chart and interpreted according to the level of suffering.

• • •

Box #9 – Family roots

Sense of family roots

Imagine two people, whom we will call Joseph and Nicholas. Joseph lives in a house. His brother lives on the first floor, and his mom lives on the second floor. His cousin lives down the street as does his mother-in-law. His uncle is going to buy an apartment close to all of them, because he feels his house, which is located 10 km away, seems too far. The family members check in 10 times a day with one another to see who is doing what and where they're doing it. At Christmas, they usually book a restaurant where everyone can celebrate together. When someone gets married, more than 300 people attend, and they're not all family members. Unfortunately, when someone gets sick, the whole family races to the hospital to see what happened leaving the doctor confused about whom to address.

And Nicholas? 18 years ago, he left home to travel abroad. Two years later, he returned, but chose to live in a city 300 km away from his mother and father's house. When he got married, he didn't notify any of his family members. Once a month, he calls his parents to chat and, sometimes, he doesn't even come home for Christmas, because he likes spending the holidays, one year at the beach and the next in the mountains. If he gets ill, he doesn't always notify his parents. He doesn't like to worry them with his problems; besides, they may not do anything for him. He reaches out to his sister from time to time by telephone and, if he goes through his hometown, he may call his brother at the last minute to see if he'd like to grab a coffee. This usually gets him scolded because he never plans ahead. Uncle or aunt? He doesn't even remember how many uncles and aunts he has. And it's been nine years since he's seen any of his cousins.

I've used two extremes. Which do you think is right and which is wrong? You are used to judging these types of situations according to your beliefs, according to your criteria. In fact, there is no "right" or "wrong." Both are fine. We absolutely don't want to say that Joseph loves his family more than Nicholas. In life, we encounter both of these situations among people we know. Our duty is not to judge them but accept them as they are. That's the beauty of life. Each of us is different; each of us lives our own life as he sees fit. And now let's find out how to recognize the level of the sense of family and roots.

If there is no digit in box number 9

These people have a free spirit and are not particularly connected to their family of origin. We often hear them explain that their families are people who love them and not necessarily the people whom they want to spend time with. That does not mean they do not love their families, it just simply means they don't feel obliged to stay close to them.

Observation: From 1900 until 1999, we always found at least one number 9 in everyone's date of birth. On the birthdates of people born after 2000, that is no longer the case. To that end, please know that to raise children born between 1900 to 1999 is totally different than raising those who were born from 2000 onward. Those born in the twentieth century always have a tendency to inculcate in the minds of their children the traditions, family habits, rules, and in some sense to force their children to follow the old ways.

Those born from 2000 on have a tendency to raise their children in complete freedom, favoring them to make their own choices, choose their own path, somehow allowing children to decide for themselves. They live like this, but they cannot express themselves freely. Their rigid parents or grandparents were born in 1900; their perception of the family is different.

A single digit in box number 9 (9)

These people are freethinking. They are people who love their family but who don't feel a great obligation to spend every Sunday with them. They are not bound by tradition in any particular way. They can celebrate Christmas where they want, one year in the mountains and the other at the sea. When a person with one digit in box number 9 becomes a parent, they will be a very easy-going parent. Very quiet, allowing freedom to their child. Unfortunately, however, these people don't always listen or understand their role as a parent, and they may abandon their children or live their whole life trying to learn how to become a good parent.

Two digits in box number 9 (99)

These people already feel a deep obligation to their family of origin. They give priority to their entire family: mother, father, husband, wife, children, but they often can forget about themselves, without realizing that they have to feel good and be well first. Then they can make those around them feel good.

Three digits in box number 9 (999)

Here we see a great desire to be close to family. The importance of family runs deep in these people. If they live far away or a death occurs in the family, it generally takes a lot more time, sometimes a lifetime, to process the pain. As parents, they are very protective, sometimes overly so because they obsessively want to prevent every hardship, obstacle, or challenge their child might encounter. If they could, they would roll out a red carpet in front of them so they could easily stroll through life, avoiding pain and suffering. Unfortunately, they do not realize that by doing so, they are just manipulating, and that, instead of protecting them, they are doing harm. For when the child grows up, he will have a difficult time facing the inconveniences of life, and he will struggle to manage them. When people with three digits in box number 9 become attached to you and include you in their extended family, you will forever be a part of their inner circle.

Four or more digits in box number 9 (9999)

These people live and breathe family. Being an individual comes second to being a part of their family. For them, it is the most important thing in life. They can live for generations in the same house or in the same way or at least in the same town.

Observation

With the name "family," it also includes a created family or a chosen family. A group of friends, or work colleagues, or perhaps an association can form their own family. People who have more numbers 9, and who for some reason are unable to create a traditional family, become attached to these types of groups as a way of replacing a traditional family.

In the number 9 section, you've learned the importance of knowing how many number 9's are in the chart of the table of THE SECRET of NUMBERS.

However, this box is to be read in conjunction with energies of the other numbers and, based on this, the level of sense of the family that is experienced.

• • •

We continue in the explanation of the other numbers in the table.

How to fill in the boxes at the end of the three horizontal lines.

The meaning of the box
at the end of the first horizontal line.

Here is the explanation about how you calculate the empty box at the end of the first horizontal line: count the total number of digits (consider only the digits in the row and not their numerical value). The significance of this box is determination, and it is determined on a scale from 1 (lowest) to 9 (highest).

Determination

An individual's determination is closely linked to his tendency for procrastination. There have been many books written about this. For this reason, a long and detailed conversation about this will not be discussed here. Rather, I want to share with you my point of view.

Every thought in our head requires a certain amount of energy to think. Therefore, every time we think about something we need to do, in a certain way, it uses valuable brainpower and can block a bit of our energy. When the number of things we need to do increases, of course, we must allocate more of our internal energy resources to them.

Thoughts, such as: "After I finish doing that, then I'll do this other thing. Then tomorrow I will schedule this... then that." and on it goes. This ongoing list of things to do running in the background of our mind does nothing but create tension. It requires large blocks of energy to think about. Naively and unrealistically, we continue to tell ourselves that we'll have enough time to accomplish everything, and we think we can stretch out time like a superhero. However, there is a but... But in reality, do we honestly have enough time to accomplish all of it? Take the time to reflect on just how much time it actually took us to accomplish these things in the past. Accept the limitations with how much we can honestly cram into the time we have. I know it's hard to admit, but it's true.

Imagine how freeing it would feel if one day you were presented with a specific thing to do, and you were able to get busy working on it right away, because you were not overwhelmed with a million other commitments taking chunks of your precious energy. Wouldn't that be wonderful to have your thoughts and energy automatically start flowing? Is it possible to remain ready and relaxed while thinking about many other things? When you embrace this concept, and apply it in your everyday life, it will soon become apparent that you are proceeding step by step towards your goal. You're finally going in the direction you've always wanted. Suddenly, a realization of not being blocked comes over you, a feeling of fluidity, of freedom, at last more consistent, stable, and patient.

This is because patience and perseverance are related to procrastination. Others will notice it, because patience isn't automatic, nor is it constant. A majority of people are shortsighted, wanting everything immediately, at the expense of the determination.

The scale of the determination in the people is interpreted in the following ways:

1 – Unfortunately this type of person cannot carry out any actions that needs to be done without constant reminding and encouragement. They have a strong tendency to postpone commitments, even those of everyday life. One of their strengths is seeing the needs of others and helping. But helping others shouldn't be their priority; they should help themselves first. Unfortunately, they don't concern themselves with what they should do.

2 – Here we again hear more talk than action. Even this person takes great effort to achieve anything without being reminded and encouraged. Their determination is low with a great propensity to procrastinate.

3 – Here is where we begin to see commitment come into the picture. But, in the end, this person tends to put things off without realizing it. Not all the time, but excuse making does creep in. They justify reasons why it's acceptable to wait in fulfilling their obligations in the present moment. If in the end, they fail to complete their commitment, the real reason is their lack of determination. It would be enough to admit their shortcomings to themselves and ask for help from someone who will hold them account-able on a daily basis, checking to see if they did what they said they would.

4 – Here determination begins to solidify into form. It's no longer just words. Goals and objectives are achieved and completed although they come at slow speeds. Number 4 people have a tendency to complete things

but often at the last minute. This fact, of course, torments them inside with inner turmoil and guilt.

5 – These people always do what they set out to do. Steady, stable, and consistent, they pursue an aim to its end, following through every step of the way. At times, they may be slow, but still they never give up or quit; these people have great determination.

6 – Number 6's always finish what they say they're going to do. We don't hear a lot of promises without them being followed up by facts. Rarely is it seen in these people that they make a commitment and then postpone it, or worse, don't follow it through to the end. Gasp, they couldn't live with themselves if that happened.

7 – Here we see a high level of determination, that at times, it is so high that the possibility of not achieving it becomes very real.

8 – The motto of number 8's is: "execute, produce, realize." They get their stuff done. The only thing you must realize is that some are a little slower than others. We can't say they are slow, just that they do things more slowly. It must not always be expected that everyone will perform at the same speed as others. Here, determination is very high. These people never see obstacles in the realization of anything.

9 – Their determination is through the roof!

Observation

The box of determination must be read along with the energies of the other numbers. In doing so, we can see a robust group of people who, when they need to bring something to an end for themselves, are determined. However, when doing things for others, they tend to postpone their completion.

• • •

The meaning of the box
at the end of the second horizontal line

Remember when calculating the empty box at the end of the second horizontal line: count the total number of digits (consider only the digits in the row and not their numerical value). The significance of this box is sensitivity, and it is determined on a scale from 1 (lowest) to 9 (highest).

Awareness/Sensitivity

What do I mean by the word sensitivity? Often people say, "I am very sensitive, and people take advantage of me." The truth is that highly sensitive individuals are not even capable of expressing how they feel or describing their feelings, emotions, and the constant turmoil they feel within them to others. Sensitive people hide how they feel, retreating inside themselves without saying a word or talking too much as a means of hiding their true feelings.

More than other people, those who are sensitive have the capacity to capture a gesture, a look, a smile, a word, subtle nuances (good and evil, happiness and sadness, love or hate) that those less sensitive would never perceive. Sensitivity does not mean fragility. Rather, it is a characteristic of force, giving insight to others. Sensitive people are readily able to express themselves through art or to use it to understand others. In today's society, it's a great gift.

The scale of the sensitivity in the people is interpreted in the following ways:

0 – This is a very rare phenomenon! And when it occurs, we find ourselves confronted by people who have separated their heart from their mind. They somehow believe they struggle to "feel" although they may seem affectionate, cute, can sometimes speak of love and peace. However, they simply say it out loud as a means of convincing themselves that they can feel. However, if you are having a difficult time, in tense situations, or in the middle of a discussion with a zero, their natural coldness can sometimes strike fear into the hearts of others.

1, 2 – People like this are detached, cold people. Their language can sometimes be harsh, but they don't even realize their words can wound like arrows. In dealing with a difficult situation, these people can dissociate so much that they may appear to be uninterested in what is happening around them. These people don't particularly like physical contact.

3 – This type of person can easily adjust his feelings, but in the same way he is often capable of cutting straight to the heart of the matter with indifference and detachment. At times, it may appear that they are not even present or paying attention to what is happening.

4, 5 – Here, we begin to see more sensitive people. A gesture as small as a word or a look can move them to tears. Physical contact is necessary to these people. Sometimes they show a false "coldness" or act like they don't care for other people, because they're so afraid of getting hurt. Actually, there is a volcano inside of them that cries out, wanting to be accepted and understood.

6, 7, 8, 9 – Moving higher on the scale, the characteristics as described in the previous rows increase more and more. Here, we find extremely sensitive people who live and perceive reality through their emotion or feelings. If they'd allow their protective barrier of fear to drop, perhaps of being hurt to empathize with others immediately, they'd be helping themselves so much.

In this section about sensitivity, you've learned to understand why it is important to know the number of digits in the box of sensitivity in of the table of THE SECRET of NUMBERS.

However, this box should always be read in conjunction with the energies of the other numbers.

• • •

The meaning of the box at the end of the third horizontal row.

The significance of this box is intelligence.

Remember when calculating the empty box at the end of the third horizontal row: count the total number of digits (consider only the digits in the row and not their numerical value). The significance of this box is intelligence, and it is determined on a scale from 1 (lowest) to 9 (highest).

Intelligence

One may think that the meaning of this word is obvious. But I'd like you to reflect on its meaning for a second. I think there are two types of intelligences: the first one is called the science of the brain, and the second one is called the wisdom of the soul. One must never confuse the two or put them in the same category. People who have spent a great deal of their lives studying, reading, debating with friends, equipping themselves with the latest information, attending many courses, filling their homes with of books of all kinds, receiving relevant diplomas, and, when asked any question, know the answer to any question on any subject like a living encyclopedia, are people linked to the **Science of the brain**. They completely identify with their brains and retain all the knowledge from all the books they've ever read. However, they are not necessarily the most intelligent. Because when you ask a question of them to express an opinion on a subject connected to life, to feeling, to the invisible, to not be measured, this can throw them for a loop. Their knowledge is linked to remembering facts and figures they've read in books or studied. These people often feel like they don't know enough; thus, they continue to fill their minds with more information, hoping that one day they finally will know everything.

On the contrary, there are people who didn't do well in school, they never cracked open a book, and rarely attended class. When you ask them something about a topic with which they weren't familiar, it wouldn't bother them in the slightest not to know the answer, because they'd know where to go to find out. They wouldn't be ashamed at all if they didn't know dates of wars, or specific names of prominent figures, from memory. However, when you ask them anything to do with life, feeling, or the invisible, they are capable of speaking about it with great confidence, peace, and inner calm.

Wisdom of the soul

We can easily identify people with high intelligence. This can be perhaps a great scientist, who doesn't have an introspective view of life. And then upon closer examination, despite never having read a book in his life, we encounter a person who knows more than the person with three degrees hanging on his wall.

With this, we do not want to diminish the importance of study or education. I would just like to point out the difference between the two. If your brother has three degrees, and you don't even have one, it does not mean he's smarter than you.

And going still deeper into this topic.

Why do people keep studying? Because they want to know more; because they want to find answers to their questions; because they always want to be ready with the right answer in every situation, and that's why they never stop searching. But there is a but. But this does not stop in the study involving the use of energy – the ever present energy that continually flows to and through you.

Stop for a three day period – do not study, do not read, do not watch TV, and do not listen to the radio. You will begin to see what happens. Slowly, you will feel this energy emerge. At first, it would be on the surface, caused by particular sensations, and feelings of tranquility pass over you. Feelings that you're ready to understand more things than you could ever imagine.

This is my point of view about intelligence.

I would like to point out that the average intelligence is a 2.

1, 2 – These people are simple. They have their way of thinking, and they struggle to get to the bottom of things, preferring instead to keep their conversations superficial. They don't particularly like to study, read, or think for long periods. Before reaching a conclusion on a subject, they may need to put a lot more time than others; therefore, they need to surround themselves with people who are patient with them. This does not mean they are stupid people by any means. They just don't feel the need to become walking encyclopedias.

3 – Here we begin to see people with whom you can discuss a more diverse number of topics. They want to understand more about you, and they like a deeper engagement and challenge when it comes to conversations.

4, 5 – Now we see the intelligence level rising. Number 4 and 5's are people who like to get to the bottom of things, to analyze them. Keeping current is an important part of their lives. But we must remember not to fill their heads and minds for the sole purpose of information gathering without ever putting it into practice. These people probably sense that what they've studied isn't all that exists, and that not all answers are found in books. These answers are also found by listening to their inner voices and relying on the wisdom of their souls.

6 – Here intelligence levels rise even more. These people are beginning to be so smart that we may begin to see those who, if they understand their high intelligence, could potentially manipulate others to get what they want.

A little note about manipulation – it is possible for manipulation to be used both positively and negatively, depending on the level of a person's intelligence and how they wield its power. It all depends on the person.

7 – These people are really smart! Their intelligence goes even one step beyond what I wrote about the 4's, 5's and 6's. At times, their high intelligence can turn into an obstacle, disconnecting them from the "real" world.

8 – Here we find a very high level of intelligence. Even though these people are in possession of great minds. At times though, it can actually be a hindrance, creating problems for them. In fact, more to the point, they have a desire to analyze and investigate everything, and constant turning of their mental wheel prevents them from turning off their brains. For number 8's, learning how to relax is imperative for living a peaceful life. They must learn to give their minds a respite from thinking and analyzing. If not, their system can become overwhelmed to the point of exhaustion by the constant stream of thoughts that arise.

9 – Genius

In this section about intelligence, you've learned to understand why it is important to know the number of digits in the box of intelligence in the table of THE SECRET of NUMBERS. However, this box should always be read in conjunction with the energies of the other numbers.

• • •

The meaning of the box
at the bottom of the first column.

The significance of this box is talent/artistry.

Remember when calculating the empty box at the bottom of the first column: count the total number of digits (consider only the digits in the column and not their numerical value). The significance of this box is talent and artistry, and it is determined on a scale from 1 (lowest) to 9 (highest).

The average talent/artistry is 5.

Talent/Artistry

Often, when you hear the word talent, what comes to mind is success linked to earning great amounts of money or to have extraordinary ability for those who possess it. When you hear the word "artistry," your ideas are most likely confused, because you probably think it's necessary to work with your hands and far from thought. Artistry is an expression of creative thought manifested into material form through a variety of practical skills such as drawing, painting, sculpting, carving, whittling, writing, or sewing, as well as gardening, cooking, or participating in sports of all types. Then there are the talents where artistry is useless, but this absolutely does not mean that the person is not creative. These talents which I call "talents of thought" express themselves through the mental faculties of speaking, teaching, motivating, listening, memorizing, imagining, innovating, proposing, and reciting.

To this, we must get rid of the old idea that those who aren't creative or artistic are devoid of talent.

When we hear about those who have talent or artistic skills, we often assume they have something extra or something special beyond what normal people possess. It's not uncommon to believe that exceptional talent is the prerogative to being a great man and woman. This is incorrect!

Every single person has a talent, a gift, or something special that marks him as unique and impossible to duplicate. Unfortunately, we've been raised in a society where our tendency to compare ourselves with others dominates.

Why do adults feel obliged to encourage their children to pick their talent so early? But which one should a child choose if they are good at many? What parents and schools believe is the "right" talent may not be the one the child is best at or enjoys the most. Perhaps a child at such a young age can't express his wishes to pursue something he loves out of fear, or people pleasing, or for whatever reason. Then, unfortunately, the parents don't think to encourage what it is that child loves, and somehow it gets lost, or it's never pursued. Until 25 years later, when a hidden, suppressed, or previously undiscovered talent emerges, his proficiency in it surprises and amazes everyone. Most often, the one who is the most surprised and amazed by their newfound talent is the one who is doing it!

From an early age, schoolteachers pretended that all their pupils were talented at drawing, jumping, writing, counting, singing, dancing, and talking, mostly to keep order in the classroom, rather than developing the unique and special talents of each child.

As Albert Einstein said, "Everyone is a genius. But if you judge a fish by its ability to climb a tree, it will live its whole life believing that it is stupid."

People's talent/artistry is interpreted in the following ways:

1, 2, 3 – These are the people who do not like manual labor and have no particular artistic skills. They would never sit down, pick up a paintbrush, and start painting a picture, nor would they fix something that is broken at home; they prefer to call a specialist in to make the repair. There are women who avoid housework or who don't like to cook. They usually require a lot of help. This type of person is usually more inclined to have stronger mental faculties.

4 – Number 4's do a few things with their hands, but they are still people who avoid using them if at all possible. They may possess a variety of special talents; however, here they may have a greater tendency to have, as I called them, "talents of thought."

5 – Here we encounter those people who work well with their hands and enjoy the act of using them. Generally speaking, they are individuals who can perform a task with confidence, speed, and commitment. These people never hesitate in doing manual labor. They roll up their sleeves and get busy, doing whatever is necessary to get the job done.

6, 7 – These people possess above average talents. They may excel in singing, drawing, acting, or many other types of activities. Often they have a predisposition to both manual skills and intellectual talents. They are very creative and, in their hands, things seem to move on their own as if by magic.

8, 9 – These people have "golden hands" and excellent talents. They tend to be healers, artists, painters, architects, singers, writers, dancers, and athletes. Their abilities are elevated to a point where they actually manage to move others emotionally, and they should always spend the time to fully develop them. Often, these people get stuck because, in fact, they are good at doing so many things, they have a tough time choosing just one and, for this reason, they often become paralyzed and end up doing nothing. We should encourage them to focus on the talent that brings them the most joy.

In this section about talent and artistry, you've learned to understand why it is important to know the number of digits in the box of talent and craftsmanship in the table of THE SECRET of NUMBERS. However, this box should always be read in conjunction with the energies of the other numbers.

• • •

The meaning of the box at the bottom of the second column

The significance of this box is confidence in self and others.

Remember when calculating the empty box at the bottom of the second column: count the total number of digits (consider only the digits in the column and not their numerical value). The significance of this box is confidence in self and others, and it is determined on a scale from 1 (lowest) to 9 (highest).

Confidence in self and others

In my view, this is one of the most important features on the entire table. Because as one sees and judges himself, a value is assigned based on how much trust he has in himself.

Unfortunately, many of us have problems with our self-confidence. This lack of good self-esteem begins at a young age. Not all of us were lucky enough to have parents or teachers who were encouraging and positive with us. In fact, so many of us experienced a similar situation in which the predominant tendency of our elders was to focus on what we weren't doing well, ending in scolding or spanking. Compliments for a job well done may have even been a rarity, if they happened at all. So our self-esteem got worse and worse. If you reflect on it for a moment, under circumstances like those, where do we place our trust?

Belief in ourselves, in our value, and feeling confident helps us to meet the challenges and opportunities in life with more strength and resilience. The more self-confidence we have, the more we feel the need to express our inner wealth with others.

The lower the confidence we have in ourselves, the more limited our goals will be, even making their achievement unlikely. If we don't trust ourselves, our abilities, and our way of being, we will certainly have a tendency to approach life with more difficulties. If you have low self-esteem, it becomes increasingly hard to pursue your ideas, express your feelings, or enter into relationships with others. If we lack confidence in ourselves, we will be more apt to base our own value on the opinions of others, leading us away from our true selves.

Self-confidence also involves a profound ability to accept when you are living harmoniously with others. We don't expect others to do anything for us which instills in us a sense of self-reliance, filling us with an inner confidence. If I trust myself, I trust in others.

It is, in fact, the difference between being open and receptive or closed and unaccepting about the world around us.

The scale of confidence in self and others is interpreted in the following ways:

0 – These people are deeply insecure. They don't trust themselves, nor do they trust anyone else. Initially, they may not seem insecure at all, trying to appear the opposite. They create a false persona behind which they hide, trying to convince themselves that they really are who they are pretending to be. They act like they're a strong person, full of confidence, wearing this fake mask whenever they're in the midst of other people. These people can come across as very arrogant, but this is nothing more than a way to hide their insecurity. Their whole life is lived with the deep conviction that you cannot trust anybody, and that everybody is out to get them. This leads them to turn inward to live a life of profound loneliness and isolation. They find it hard to open up to others and to let loose.

1, 2 – At this point, a little trust in themselves and others begins to present itself but in small amounts. In any case, they continue to feel as if they constantly live in the spotlight and often act accordingly even though they never really have because they constantly fear being judged by others. And, alternatively, they tend to judge others as a means of getting in front of the judgment of others, all the while hiding behind their own insecurities.

3 – Here we begin to see self-confident people with an even stronger confidence in others.

4 – These people have a level of self-confidence that is high, and they trust in others. However, they often tell others more about themselves and their lives than is necessary. They should learn to curb their sharing and understand that they must not tell everything about themselves on a first date. The date won't find all this information particularly interesting. Sometimes, others may consider their friendly and outgoing way as being naive. It can lead number 4's to being misunderstood.

5, 6, 7, 8, 9 – Here we find people who put a lot of trust in themselves and others. They should be more careful about telling their own personal things to others, because oftentimes, they trust too much and then are surprised when what they shared is used against them. Naively, they believe others live and share as openly and freely as they do, but that is just not so.

In this section about confidence in self and others, you've learned to understand why it is important to know the number of digits in the box of confidence in self and others in the table of THE SECRET of NUMBERS. However, this box should always be read in conjunction with the energies of the other numbers.

• • •

The meaning of the box
at the bottom of the third column.

The significance of this box is materialism/speech.

Remember when calculating the empty box at the bottom of the third column: count the total number of digits (consider only the digits in the column and not their numerical value). The significance of this box is materialism/speech, and it is determined on a scale from 1 (lowest) to 9 (highest).

Materialism

Materialism is a characteristic of a person who tends to seek not only goods and pleasures but also material things. This strongly influences their behavior. Materialistic people base their existence on what they have, continuously measuring their possessions. Their mood and level of happiness changes, depending on their results. Things become the substance of their lives, and they cannot imagine a future without obtaining more of them. Materialism is the prison that locks people into a completely limited world, which separates the finite from the infinite.

The materialism scale is interpreted in the following ways:

0 – People who cannot see beyond matter. Their state is constantly changing, because it is strongly linked to external things. These people need to be surrounded by "things" and give value to themselves only according to

what they have. Unfortunately, they also evaluate others on the same basis. Easily excited for one thing, once they have it, they quickly lose interest in it; and they chase after their next thing. These people are very dependent on material things and often continue to buy more and more "things" for no reason.

1, 2 – These people are highly materialistic with a tendency to rejoice when they come back with a bag full of new things. These people become overprotective toward their belongings, because protecting their things is related to possessiveness. They say to themselves, "I'm afraid someone will steal something from me." They may base their entire self-worth, self-confidence, and safety on owning that thing. Of course, it scares them to lose any of their possessions. They're afraid of losing anything, because "it would take away a piece of me."

3, 4 – Number 3's & 4's are beginning to understand and, above all, see beyond matter and materialism. They understand they cannot base their life on only one thing. Also, they do like to surround themselves with "beautiful things," but they are aware that the things are not an important thing in their lives.

5, 6, 7 – These people are not interested in the material world. This does not mean that they don't own anything. Or maybe they don't work to have expensive things. The important criterion is how they perceive the world, how living things from here are around them. They usually have a special relationship with the material world. On one hand, they like nice things and on the other hand, they realize they don't need them either.

8, 9 – People like this are completely detached from the material world; it has no meaning for them in the least.

Speech

It's the way you speak and how easily you express yourself with words clearly and with great linguistic finesse.

The speech scale is interpreted in the following ways:

0, 1, 2 – These people observe more and talk less. They often don't speak unless they're invited to do so and at times may seem quiet. This, however, does not mean that they are embarrassed, or that they have nothing to say.

3, 4 – When these people are in groups, they want to speak, to share their ideas and to have their say. I suggest that if you meet people who have more of a tendency to be quiet, to invite them to speak, because they often have much more to say than those who talk all the time.

5, 6, 7 – Here, we have people with a tendency to speak a lot. Sometimes, they do not even realize that they shouldn't talk about someone else. They have this gift with which they can get what they want when their speech is used in a positive way. They are a good candidate for any of the following professions: speaker, teacher, journalist, lawyer, actor, etc.

8, 9 – You can never say a single word in the company of these people. They absolutely take advantage of their great gift for gab (blah, blah, blah ...).

In this section about materialism/speech, you've learned to understand why it is important to know the number of digits in the box of materialism/speech in the table of THE SECRET of NUMBERS. However, this box should always be read in conjunction with the energies of the other numbers.

With this description, we have finished the explanation of the boxes in the table. Now, let's talk about reading the numbers in combination. Let's show you the importance of always considering every aspect of your chart simultaneously, in conjunction with all the numbers, not just individually. Because individual numbers will tell you a single feature, but looking simultaneously at the other numbers will tell you other equally important things.

However, every box, even though I have already repeated it many times, is always read in conjunction with the other boxes and their numbers.

• • •

Combination boxes

As you know, up until now, I have illustrated and explained the meaning of each box of the table. Even more extraordinarily, "my" interpretation of this ancient instrument is determined by the fact that you can interpret a combination of several boxes together. This way, you can get a reading from which emerges many other valuable morsels of information about a person.

Below, I will explain the meaning of some very significant combinations, though they are only a small number of the many possible combinations that can be interpreted from the table.

Combining boxes to gain clarity on their interpretation:

Box number 2 is closely linked to box number 4. If you have no numbers in box number 2 and no numbers in box number 4, you should be very careful about your health. You can be vulnerable because you are weak physically and frequently encounter diseases. The advice I want to give you is to pay close attention to your nutrition, your physical activity, and your lifestyle to minimize the possibility of your getting sick.

For those of you who do have numbers in both boxes 2 & 4, you're not to worry. If you do have numbers in both of these boxes in your table, and you get sick often, it's because you worry too much. To heal your frequent illnesses, pay particular attention to what you're thinking about. If you begin to become aware of your negative thoughts and change them to positive ones, you'll recover faster from your illnesses.

In addition, if you have no numbers 2, 4, or 8 in your table, you are prone to having not only physical illnesses but also psychological ones such as: anxiety, stress, and depression, as well a whole host of other mental diseases. You must pay close attention to taking good care of yourself.

If you have no numbers in box number 2, but there are numbers in both box numbers 4 & 8, or if you have no numbers in box number 8, but you have numbers in box numbers 2 & 4, when engaged in intimate relationships, you don't particularly enjoy having sex. Instead of doing the act for the end result of having an orgasm, you enjoy the mental, sentimental, and emotional part as an enhancement to the physical part. Basically, you prefer foreplay instead of sex.

Now let's take a look at the determination box at the end of the first horizontal line and interpret it together.

If your table has no numbers in box number 4, and the total number in the determination box is equal to 1, 2, or 3, there is a strong probability that you are susceptible to addictions (smoking, alcohol, drugs, sex, adrenaline, money, etc...)

In many cases, you may not even be aware that you suffer from addictive tendencies. Intervention from an outside source may be needed to not only identify the addiction but also to help treat it. Oftentimes, your willpower is too low and isn't strong enough to beat your addiction.

Another very important interpretation to analyze in the table is the combined reading of box numbers 5 & 7. If you have both numbers in both of these boxes, then you are equipped with intuition combined with spirituality. You have a predisposition for spirituality to become your life mission. If there are no numbers in either boxes number 5 & 7, no one is more tied to the material world. Concepts such as spirituality and intuition may seem completely foreign to you.

If you have a number in box number 6, you may be a strongly undecided person unless you also have a number in box number 5. In that case, you will use your intuition to make your decisions; the more 5's in that box, the more you will use your intuition in your decision making. Therefore, in some way, having a number 5 rescues you if you don't have a number 6. My advice to a person like this is to trust your inner voice. Your intuition will guide you to make the right choices.

If the table has neither number 5 or 6, and you are a successful person, you must take a look at box number 1 (ego) to see how many number 1's you have. If there are three or more number 1's, this means that you make all your decisions relying solely on your mind. Since the mind is closely tied to the ego, your decisions most likely don't take into consideration the benefits and happiness of others. It is because your decisions are made solely by using pure ego and are linked exclusively to your own welfare, without regard to the benefit of others.

Now you have learned about cross reading of various boxes and how they can change the overall interpretation of someone's table. If you were to stretch the table and associate the reading of individual boxes with those of other boxes, they would slowly start to tell a story; a story that would speak of the intricacies of a single table; a story that would talk about a single date of birth; a story that would recount the tendencies and idiosyncrasies of an individual person. And this information is really wonderful to have. Just reflect on how gathering this information, and gaining a new awareness from this amazing world of numbers, can help each of us. It is a subject that I love very much.

Do you recognize the importance of this?

Does it intrigue you?

The numbers really have so much to say that I wanted to share the information with you as well as provide you with some examples that bring it more to life!

• • •

Conclusion

Welcome

I want to congratulate you, because you belong to a special group of people who now understand. You understand why I said that the book didn't drop into your hand by accident. Now you understand that there are no accidents; they don't exist. I am proud of you for not putting it back on the shelf or letting it sitting unread on the bedside table or returning it to the library. Basically, you haven't let the dust settle on the cover. Instead, you started and finished reading it all the way to the end. Bravo!

And because of your persistence, you have now discovered that it is an incredible tool that must be protected, preserved, and disseminated everywhere. It is an ancient instrument that was hidden from view for thousands of years. Maybe you initially thought this book would be like a simple fortune telling normally found in a newspaper or a magazine. Maybe you did not even realize the immense importance and value its great heritage would give you.

Now you've learned to analyze your own date of birth, you've learned to count with numbers that compose it, and you've learned to build yourself an exceptional table that told you about YOU.

By reading this book, you have acquired a new perspective about life. You have become aware that the numbers that make up your date of birth are not just numbers but they are important advisers. They are messengers that help you to better understand about you and the people around you.

Each of us is different; no two people are alike. We take this for granted. And there is a beauty in that. With the information contained in this book, you have learned to examine in detail what the differences really are that distinguish one person from another. It's as if you have been given a new set of eyes with which to see beyond the surface, beyond the mask, to see past what it is that other people want to show. It's wonderful, isn't it?

And you can now count yourself among those who have found the courage to continue beyond the surface and overcome your prejudices against the invisible world of numbers!

• • •

And now?

Today's society needs to be healed, it needs to be saved in some way, it needs a helping hand, it needs "someone" with "something" to help it! And the truly amazing thing is that "someone" is really you. Finally, with your new knowledge of the table of THE SECRET of NUMBERS, you can contribute to its improvement. This is true, trust me.

So what now?

It depends on whether you seize the importance of this message – that the numbers of birth dates can find answers to your deepest questions. It's up to you to realize the opportunity that life has presented to you.

Decide if you will immediately begin to apply the knowledge you've acquired

If you choose yes, immediately put down the book, take out a notebook and pen and write the first and last names of the five people you care most. Alongside their names, write their birth dates. As soon as you've finished reading the last few pages, get to work building their tables, entering in the numbers into the boxes. Once the table is filled in, begin to understand how they are so you can improve your approach toward them.

I strongly recommend you buy yourself a notebook and every time you analyze a date of birth, write it there, so all the analyzed tables remain united. Also, write your name, email address, and phone number on the inside cover, so if you ever misplace it, whoever finds it can contact you and return it to you.

Why should you do this? There are two reasons. One is that, by doing so, you will continuously have the chance of reviewing the tables of various people you know to understand them better and more deeply. Their numbers will confirm what you've learned in this book. The second reason is that I want you to thank each table you build and analyze. Yes, you read that correctly. I want you to thank each table, with great respect, for the messages it communicated to you. Every time I finish a reading, I close my eyes for a moment and quietly say, "Thank you."

And if this magnificent world of numbers has intrigued you more than expected, and you want to develop it even further by learning more details about the interpretation of the chart, I invite you to visit our website www.thesecretofnumbers.com. There, you will find updates on our activities, video courses, live classes, and more. You will also find my first book for purchase, which I strongly recommend you read. Again, it is currently available only in Italian.

Together with Andrea, I decided, after many requests, to open up a school to teach in detail this unique system of interpretation of the table of the SECRET of THE NUMBERS. We want to train future teachers who learn it on a deep level to help us disseminate it properly around the world. The importance and usefulness of this ancient instrument will be able to help those in our society who are "getting sick" every day. If YOU want to become one of our teachers, I'd love to meet you in person, look into your eyes, and shake your hand. And maybe take a peek at your birthdate.

• • •

A new pair of eyes

Why do I use the expression a new set of eyes? Because if you reflect upon it, now you are able to see beyond the superficial, and with the energy behind the numbers, you are able to see birthdates in a completely new and different way. From now on, use the "new eyes" you've acquired through the study of this book in every moment of your life!

The ancient knowledge hidden within the table of THE SECRET of NUMBERS will allow you to improve the quality of your life. Know that your table represents a precise roadmap about you and your inner world with all the various traits of your personality. Now you can better understand not only yourself, but also the people you care about the most, like your family, partner, friends, or work colleagues. Once you know how they think and what goes on in their heads, you can dramatically improve your communication and establish more harmonious relationships with them. If you commit to using the system, your results will be amazing. THE SECRET of NUMBERS can become your secret weapon to living the life of your dreams. I hope you understand that I am not exaggerating this fact one bit!

It is now a time you can ill afford to say, "That happened because of this," or "This happened because of that." You can no longer say, "She's so strange! She looked at me wrong," or "I cannot stand the way she acts." NOT ANYMORE! Not now that you know this information. Because if you do it again, if you allow yourself to think this thought, you have not fully understood the importance of this book. It means you are still "imprisoned" by judgment. It means that if you still worry about being judged by others, you were probably not ready to receive the subtle message that I wanted to convey.

This book has a big goal. In fact, it is practically a duty to help people break free from prisons of their own making before they hurt themselves or those around them. I hope this book will open the door to your personal freedom, to improve your ability to love your neighbor unconditionally, and to accept the people around you just as they are. Because every person is beautiful, special, and unique! Perhaps you're not yet convinced, and you think quietly to yourself, "What about the people who do harm to others, kill or destroy?" I know. But I firmly believe that they are special too. They've just let their heart become clouded by their upbringing, their associations, their life experiences, and a variety of unknown reasons.

This is not to say that we should not help others to improve themselves. When accepting others as they are, it becomes much easier to approach them if you have the knowledge about how they will respond to you. Once you get close to them, you could always help them to gain awareness by building a chart with their birth numbers if they want.

We were all born as innocent little children with clean hearts, minds, and souls.

If you'd like to help the world to wake up and evolve, please apply everything you've learned about the table of THE SECRET of NUMBERS immediately.

Visit our website: www.thesecretofnumbers.com to learn more.

Or write us an email: info@thesecretofnumbers.com to share with us about what happened in your life as a result of learning the information in this book.

What benefits have you encountered?

Please become familiar with following the method of using the table of birthdates.

Start writing out your goals today. Waiting until tomorrow is too late. Tomorrow is very unstable ground. The future could crumble beneath your feet right at the very moment that you're ready for takeoff. So don't delay in manifesting your dreams!

Always sow your seeds in the present, because the seeds you sow today will become your future!

Understand that even sunshine burns if you expose yourself to it for too long, and that it is better to take care of your inner garden by planting fragrant flowers.

Remember that everything that comes into your life comes for a reason, and you must live your life fully. If it makes you cry, you cry. If it makes you laugh, laugh. And above all, always give thanks and be grateful before all else, because that shows the universe that you are a wonderful person of great value with incredible strength.

The world is made up of plants, water, rocks, animals, and especially of people who communicate with one another.

And if we improve the communication skills we use between us, it will change the world!

When you're sad, nervous, insecure, or live through a difficult time in your life, what do you do most often? You close yourself in, you do not want to talk to anyone or look for your best friend, the person who will listen, advise, and help you out.

Do you think now that you've learned the table of THE SECRET of NUMBERS, YOU can become your own best friend?

And when you become your own best friend, it is a wonderful feeling because it can cause you to have peace in yourself and to feel a deep sense of freedom.

And the best part of it is that you will always have you with you; you take you with you everywhere you go!

You may wonder, "Does that mean then that I no longer need friends?" Absolutely not, but... I mean that you will be fine. It will be you who will be the one that other people will seek out when they're in need, it will be you who will provide a shoulder to cry on when someone else needs support, and it will be you who we will always have the energy to support others.

What a wonderful gift that is.

Finally, you will have reached a turning point when your days will be filled with questions like, "How can I help you?" or "What can I offer you?" or "What can I give?"

And nevermore will your days consist of questions like, "What can I get?" or "Who can I take from?" or "How can I get rich?"

And the famous I, I, I, me, me, me, everything is mine, changes into US, WE, YOU!

• • •

Final Grade: Blank

We've come to the end. And while I'm writing the last lines, I feel a deep and heartfelt gratitude toward you. Tears are running down my cheeks. At last, I have written down a part of "my knowledge," something that I have carried around with me for many years. Did I write "my knowledge?" No, no, no, it is not "my" knowledge. What I really meant to say was everyone's knowledge. I have simply been chosen as a channel through which the information flows. In fact, I had to get out of my own way to interpret one of the oldest scientific methods that ever existed on the planet Earth.

Sitting in front of me is Andrea, looking at me and smiling. There is no need for words to be exchanged; we understand each other anyway. He gets up, brings me his handkerchief, and says, "We did it!"

Now our mission has begun.

It is my and Andrea's wish for you to truly live an extraordinary life, full of love, health, and abundance. As it should be for everyone.

A life in which we create extraordinary relationships.

It starts now, from where you are!

Use what you have!

Make the most of what you can.

Thinking divides the world; feeling unites us. Now start to feel!

Have great trust in yourself, not what you think you should be, but what you are!

We thank the universe for having brought us together!

Monika Ben Thabetova and *Andrea Tonello*

Used Biography: *One, Two, Three Let's talk About You!* Monika Ben Thabetova

About the Authors

Monika Ben Thabetova was born in 1976 in the second largest city of the Czech Republic named Brno. Her family was of a multi-ethnic origin. After stints of living in Africa and the Czech Republic, she settled in Italy. At the age of 15, her mother introduced her to the table of THE SECRET of NUMBERS. After a short amount of time, it became apparent that she had an uncanny ability to uniquely interpret the ancient instrument. And so began her daily use of it to help the people around her.

Andrea Tonello was born in 1975 in a town called Malo in the province of Vicenza, Italy. For as long back as anyone could remember, everyone in his family made a living as a barber or a hairdresser. But thanks to his incredible strength of will and determination, Andrea broke the family pattern despite the strong opposition and lack of support from his father. Instead, he became a lawyer, eventually opening up his own law practice, which thrived from day one. Being financially successful gave him everything he thought he ever wanted. However, years later, Andrea experienced an "awakening" that lead him to realize that in spite of having "everything," he felt like he actually had nothing.